Speaking Up

Speaking Up

◆

How to Help the Children You Work with Who Live in Abusive Homes

Jesse Rutherford
Kathleen Nickerson, Ph.D.
Johanna S. Kim, Esq.

iUniverse, Inc.
New York Lincoln Shanghai

Speaking Up
How to Help the Children You Work with
Who Live in Abusive Homes

Copyright © 2006 by Jesse Rutherford

iUniverse books may be ordered through booksellers or by contacting:

iUniverse
2021 Pine Lake Road, Suite 100
Lincoln, NE 68512
www.iuniverse.com
1-800-Authors (1-800-288-4677)

ISBN-13: 978-0-595-38122-7 (pbk)
ISBN-13: 978-0-595-82490-8 (ebk)
ISBN-10: 0-595-38122-7 (pbk)
ISBN-10: 0-595-82490-0 (ebk)

Printed in the United States of America

Please note

1) This book is educational in nature and is not intended to replace the advice of an attorney. Although the information in this document was accurate at the time of publication, professionals using this information should bear in mind that the laws and regulations change over time and that interpretation of laws and regulations by court and administrative agencies may change from time to time. It is not possible to address all the numerous variations and interpretations of the law and regulations that exist. As such, it is the responsibility of every professional to consult with a lawyer or an experienced colleague if in need of legal or ethical advice. If you use any information in this book, it is the reader's personal and ethical responsibility to make sure that the facts and general information contained in it are applicable to his or her situation.

2) All names and quotes contained herein are the product of the authors' imaginations and are used fictitiously. Any resemblance to actual events (past, present, or future) or persons (dead, living, or not yet born) is entirely coincidental.

This book is dedicated to all of the professionals in the educational, faith, legal, medical, psychological, and child care fields who protect children every day by reporting child abuse.

"In the end, it is not the words of our enemies we will remember, but the silence of our friends."

—*Dr. Martin Luther King, Jr.*

Table of Contents

Introduction

For anyone who cares about children and the community they live in, reporting child abuse is a must. Many people who have frequent contact with children in their professions are mandated reporters of child abuse: people who must report by law. Whether you are a mandated reporter of child abuse, a concerned parent, or a caring community member, you have the ability to improve a child's life by ending child abuse.

For the past several years, we have been engaged in giving numerous public presentations on how to recognize and report child abuse and teen dating violence. In our outreach, we met many mandated reporters from a wide array of professions who were afraid to report child abuse. As time went on, we saw a clearer picture of mandated reporters' questions, worries, and concerns, and we felt compelled to address them directly and completely. We gained a deeper understanding of the confusion mandated reporters had about reporting.

We also wrote this book to explain the dynamics of child abuse and to dispel myths about abuse and the agencies that fight it. Between the three of us, we've had to make several reports of suspected abuse throughout our careers, and we understand how difficult and scary it is to do...and how necessary.

What follows is a simple handbook for anyone who might encounter child abuse that answers the wide range of questions and concerns mandated reporters have asked us in the last few years. We've included resources, activities, and a simple description of the laws regarding child abuse in all 50 states—

everything you need to know in order to report child abuse and create a safer world for the children you know.

Regards,

Jesse Rutherford
Kathleen Fee Nickerson, Ph.D.
Johanna S. Kim, Esq.

Chapter One

Why Me?

THE IMPORTANT ROLE YOU PLAY IN SHAPING A CHILD'S
SELF-IMAGE

Thousands of child abuse reports are made around the country
each day. In every city in the nation, children suffer from
physical, sexual, verbal, and emotional abuse, as well as
neglect, and many die from it. This happens right here in the
United States, one of the richest countries in the world!

The fact that these abused children live in the United States in
the 21st century may be one of the few advantages they have: we
arc fortunate to live in a time and place where there is a system
to help these kids. There is a national hotline for reporting
abuse, there are shelters for families, there are programs that

work with parents to help them better care for and nurture their children.

But all of those great services hinge on *you*. In order for the system to help kids, they have to *know* about them.

In this book, you will learn strategies for talking to parents, co-workers, bosses, and children when you suspect that a child is being abused, but above all, you must report the abuse. That is the only way abused children can reach the services they desperately need.

YOU MAY BE THE FIRST TO IDENTIFY CHILD ABUSE AND TEEN DATING VIOLENCE

The role you play as teacher, counselor, group leader, therapist, or confidant is more critical than you realize. Think back to your own childhood: do you remember your favorite teacher? How about your favorite group activity? You probably remember some of the adults from your childhood very clearly. Likewise, today you play a powerful role in shaping children's self-esteem and self-image. Your role may be even more important because you may be the only adult that an abused child can trust. In this section, we will explore how you can influence and build children's self esteem.

As you may have already noticed, you probably spend more time with some of the kids you work with than their parents do. In fact, if you work in a school or day care setting, you can probably bet on it. Statistics show that although the time fathers spend with their children is on the rise, the overall time children spend with their parents has decreased: working couples have lost over 20 hours a week of family and personal time over the last 35 years.[1] According to a 1997 study of families with working mothers, 41% of children under 5 years of age spend 35 or more hours a week in non-parental care.[2]

It's a busy life for kids today. Figure that the kids see their parents for one crazy hour in the morning-an hour of showering, eating breakfast, packing lunches, and searching for a matching shoe. After school, kids go to day care, sports, or music lessons, and still others let themselves into their house with a key. Maybe on a weekday evening, the family is all together for two hours before the kids go to bed. It's a time for dinner, homework, computers, and invariably, TV. Weekends are a bit calmer, but still see families rushing to sports matches, recitals, and other special events. This schedule just doesn't leave a lot of time for parents to pay attention to their kids.

It *does* leave plenty of time for them to interact with you, however. As kids are ferried around during this ultra-rushed age, teachers, day care providers, music and dance instructors, school nurses and counselors, and coaches see kids all day, every day. If you think a child or teen is being abused, you could be the only person who's noticed it and is in a position to do something about it.

Perhaps you chose your profession partly because you love kids. (You probably weren't motivated by the promise of a high salary!) At some point, you may have imagined yourself surrounded by happy children. In your dream, they were singing, laughing, and covering themselves and the multi-purpose room in gallons of blue paint. You can make this joyful image a reality, but only if the children are free from the fear and pain caused by abuse.

Kids are overwhelmingly helpless to get out of abusive situations on their own, even teenagers who roll their eyes at you and swear that they can handle anything by themselves. In fact, kids have told us that they are largely unable to identify abuse, even when it's blatant. Only you, the adult, have the power, foresight, and ability to recognize and respond appropriately to abuse.

LEGAL DUTIES OF MANDATED REPORTERS

In case you are still wondering why this book is important for you to read, here is yet another reason: you could have a legal duty as a mandated reporter. *Mandated reporters of child abuse and neglect are usually individuals who have frequent contact with children in their professions. Being a mandated reporter means that you have a legal duty to report child abuse and neg-lect.* Failure to report child abuse and neglect according to your mandated reporting duties could result in civil lawsuits or criminal charges. Depending upon your profession, you may be a mandated reporter. In order to determine whether you are, take a moment to look at the chart below.

Professions that must report in ALL states
Health care professionals
Mental health professionals
Social work professionals
Education/child care professionals
Law enforcement professionals

If your profession falls within any of the categories listed above, you are a mandated reporter of child abuse and neglect. *Even if your profession is not listed above, you may still be a mandated reporter if your profession requires you to have extensive contact with children.* Many states include additional professions under their mandated reporting laws. For instance, in California, clergy are mandated reporters of child abuse and neglect. For further information on additional professions with mandated reporting responsibilities, see your state's child abuse and neglect statute, or Appendix II of this book.

If you are a mandated reporter, you have a legal duty to report child abuse and neglect. This simply means that the law requires you to report child abuse and neglect to either your local child protective services (CPS) agency or law enforcement. That being said, you may be wondering *when* you should report abuse if you have a legal duty to do so. To determine when you must make a report of child abuse or neglect, look at the chart below:

Standard for making a mandated report
When you *suspect* that a child has been abused or neglected
OR when you *have reason to believe* that a child has been abused or neglected

Although this standard may vary slightly from state to state, mandated reporters generally have a legal duty to report when they either know or suspect child abuse or neglect. For further information on your state's mandated reporting standards and guidelines, see your state's child abuse and neglect statute or Appendix II. You may also visit your county or state's website or call your local law enforcement agency for more detailed information in your area.

Through your reading of this section, you may have discovered that your profession makes you a mandated reporter of child abuse and neglect. If you are a mandated reporter, you have a legal duty to report child abuse and neglect. Therefore, you *must* report any known or suspected instances of child abuse or neglect to your local CPS agency or law enforcement. Remember that when you make a report of child abuse or neglect, not only are you fulfilling your duties under the law, but you could be saving a life.[3]

LEGAL CONSEQUENCES FOR FAILURE TO REPORT:

Another important reason for getting involved is that legal penalties are imposed upon mandated reporters who don't report suspected child abuse or neglect. Almost every state in the country imposes penalties on mandated reporters who "knowingly" and/or "willfully" fail to report abuse. These penalties are usually imposed in the form of a fine, imprisonment, and in some cases both the fine and imprisonment.

Approximately 46 states have statutes that specify the penalties for failing to report child abuse or neglect. Failure to report abuse or neglect is classified as a misdemeanor, and is punishable by less than 6 months in jail in approximately 35 states. In Arizona and Illinois, subsequent violations of mandated reporter duties are classified as felonies, which are punishable by more than 6 months in jail. Therefore, if you know of or suspect abuse, you *must* report.

But It's out of My Hands!—What to Do if You're Not in Charge

Chances are, you are in no position to change the curriculum at the local high school, or to decide to spend an extra week of class talking about safety, or to change the policies at your place of work. But that doesn't mean you don't have the ability to help kids living with abuse.

What You Can Do with Adults in Your Place of Work

First of all, you *cannot* be fired for reporting suspected child abuse. If you have a reasonable suspicion of abuse and one of your superiors tells you not to report it to the authorities, report anyway. Your report remains confidential within the involved agencies; no one else has access to it. Also, as a mandated reporter, your rights are protected by law, so you can contact your local county or state bar association for low-cost legal support, or contact your union regarding your rights. This can protect you in the event that your employer should try to retaliate against you. Remember, the child is much more helpless than you are.

Let's say you haven't come across an instance of abuse at your work. You can save yourself, your co-workers, and your employers a great deal of grief by making mandated reporter duties known to them ahead of time. Many counties provide free training on mandated reporting duties to schools and other organizations who work closely with children. At the very least, you can post a child abuse reporting number in the office along with the phrase, "We are mandated by law to report suspected child abuse. If you suspect child abuse, call _____." Find your state and local numbers by searching over the internet, or see the Resources section at the back of this book.

What You Can Do with Kids

In addition, you are in complete and total control over your own actions. You can model peaceful conflict resolution and appropriate anger management strategies for your students and make your classroom, workshop area, or religious organization into a sanctuary where kids feel safe and respected.

You can also control, to some extent, the theme of materials the kids have access to. Choose plastic bowling pins over plastic guns. Books on astronauts over books on superheroes who kill and maim. Magazines on art or science over those on fashion. Magazines on the how-to aspects of music rather than those that emphasize the hedonism of music culture. Educational videos and video games that aren't built around killing or explosions.

Then, maintain close emotional contact with your students and their parents. All this means is to have frequent conversations with them. Invite older kids to analyze the world around them by asking them what they think about different issues. Build up middle school and elementary kids by praising what they do well and encouraging others to build on their good ideas. Help little ones increase their self-esteem by asking them what all their favorite things are. And share your concerns with parents not just when it's time for discipline, but when it's time for praise and at any time you think a group effort could help the child involved grow and flourish.

By making your environment a sanctuary for kids, both the kids and the parents will know you care. Parents will grow to respect and trust you more and kids will love you because they feel safe and valued in the sanctuary you have set up for them. A safe place may be the most valuable thing you can consistently offer to a child who lives in pain and fear.

How Do Children Develop Positive Self-Esteem?

When a child is born, she doesn't see herself in a good or bad way. A two-year-old doesn't say, "I'm ugly." Why not? Because everything we think when we make a judgment about something comes from our previous experiences, so without any previous experiences, we are unable to form an opinion. This is why the experiences we have in childhood and adolescence are so critical to shaping our self-esteem.

At first, the only experiences that a child has are with his family, and these experiences directly shape the child's image of himself. People who are in direct contact with a young child might immediately respond to a baby when he cries, offer soothing sounds when he becomes agitated, encourage him when he tries to walk, and praise him when he stands up alone for the first time. While each of these events on its own may not seem significant, together these actions by the child's family tell him that he is important, loved, and valued. *The feeling that you are valuable is central to the development of positive self-esteem.*

As a child grows, she will begin to have more interaction with the outside world and people, such as teachers, religious leaders, school personnel, coaches, friends, teammates, and classmates, who will help her develop self-esteem. You are one of these people! Each interaction with an adult can positively or negatively affect her self-esteem. If an experience is positive, even if the child is being disciplined, she will leave feeling accepted and valued. But if the child feels ashamed, she will probably come away with a much more negative view of herself. Repeated negative experiences result in the destruction of self-esteem. Building or preserving positive self-esteem is much easier than trying to repair low self-esteem.

Have you ever met a kid who has low self-esteem and doesn't think very highly of himself or seems to criticize herself too much? Perhaps you have a close friend who has trouble making decisions because he's so sure he will make the wrong choice. Or, maybe you've met a woman who feels she is so insignificant she repeatedly puts herself down and even engages in unhealthy behaviors because she doesn't feel worthy of success. If so, then you've seen first-hand how low self-esteem can impact someone's life—forever.

Self-Esteem Is Based on Acceptance and Success

Children learn how to behave by watching and modeling adult behavior; they see what you do, then they try to do it. Adults do this too, but for us, between observing and re-enacting there is an additional step: deciding if the behavior is desirable or not. Children have a difficult time making this decision until they have observed the outcomes of many similar decisions.

Why don't you walk across the street when the red light is flashing? Why do you call 911 in an emergency? Why don't you steal food from the store or lie to your supervisor? Because you've been in similar situations, you were told numerous ways to respond, and through repeated exposure, you've determined the best way to react. Kids need to have these teachable moments where they learn how to make these decisions for themselves and they learn most effectively when you talk about your choices and how you have made them. Your behavior is a strong influence on children's behavior and their perceptions of "acceptable" and "normal" behavior.

When an adult tells a child "Because I said so," the message is: "I am an authority, obey me," which is not a good reason from a child's perspective. Instead, try to explain your reasons for telling a child not to do something: "Drawing on the wall means we are going to have to clean it together and I think you'd have more fun playing outside instead of cleaning. So let's clean it together now and remember this next time you feel like drawing on the wall." Certainly the age of the child will determine how much you say, but whenever possible, explain your reasoning.

With teens, this can be especially challenging because adults often assume teens automatically dismiss everything we say and just do the opposite out of spite. While this may be the case some of the time, *they are often listening to you, they just don't want you to know it.* If you are concerned about a teen's desire to listen to music or watch videos that you think are destructive, instead of flat-out refusing to allow it (which rarely works—remember they have friends who have TVs), offer some counter-experiences. You might try saying, "Yes, you can have that CD, but in order to earn it, I'd like you to spend 4 hours doing volunteer work." If you feel a piece of media is much too violent for your child, you should reserve the right to not allow it, but make sure to thoroughly explain why, telling your teen "I know this is important to you, but I love you and I want the best for you. Listening to these destructive messages about women is going to be very hurtful to you when you have a relationship." Another good mantra is "I love you too much to let you do this (buy this, have this, go there, etc.)."

You are in a position to challenge the children and teens in your life and provide them with many rich learning experiences. You do this through what you say ("I love you too much to let you do this"), what you don't say ("You're stupid, not able to understand this, etc.") and most importantly, by what you do. *You absolutely must behave the way you want your children and teens to behave because otherwise your words will have no meaning and you will have zero credibility!*

If you tell kids that it is important to respect other people and then turn around and treat a co-worker with disrespect, the kids will ignore everything you say. When kids figure out that you're lying to them or just trying to keep them in line for your own convenience, they will throw out every positive learning experience they've had from you because they assume that if you lied this time, everything you do or say is probably a lie. So, you need to be very conscientious about what you say and do in the presence of children.

The good news is that there is always another day. If you behaved badly yesterday, admit it, explain why it was wrong, and tell the kids what you've done to make amends. It doesn't have to be an overly complicated explanation; it just needs to get the point across: "Yesterday I told Ms. Jones that I thought something she said was stupid, which was wrong because it hurt her feelings. I don't want her to feel bad, so I said I was sorry. I wanted you to know that I was wrong and that when you're wrong, it's important to do something to make it right."

If you consciously make an effort to turn experiences into positive teaching moments and always work towards reaffirming that the child is loved and valuable, you will do wonders for building a child's self-esteem.

Chapter Two

Why Now?

Have you ever watched the news and seen a report of abuse that has absolutely horrified you? After watching such a report, have you ever wondered, "How could this have happened?" or, "Why didn't anyone do something?" If you have, you know why it is so important for you to get involved now. When you get involved in a child's life by making a child abuse report, you play an integral role in protecting that child from future acts of abuse. By getting involved now, you have the opportunity to give a child living in an abusive environment a chance at a healthy and happy life. If that wasn't reason enough, here are some startling statistics on the prevalence of child abuse and domestic violence in the United States that may change your mind.

STATUS OF CHILD ABUSE IN THE US[4]

Child abuse and neglect is a serious problem in the United States. Here's a quick look at some of the sobering statistics:

- In 2002, an estimated 896,000 children were determined to be victims of child abuse or neglect.

- Of those 896,000 children, more than 60% experienced neglect; almost 20% were physically abused; 10% were sexually abused; and 7% were emotionally maltreated.

- Neglect is the most common form of child abuse.

- The rate of victimization per 1,000 children in the national population was 12.3 children in 2002. (According to these statistics, 12.3 children per 1,000 children in the United States are being abused.)

Below is a chart which shows the breakdown of abuse by type. Are you surprised to see which type of abuse is most common?

<u>Breakdown of abuse by type:</u>

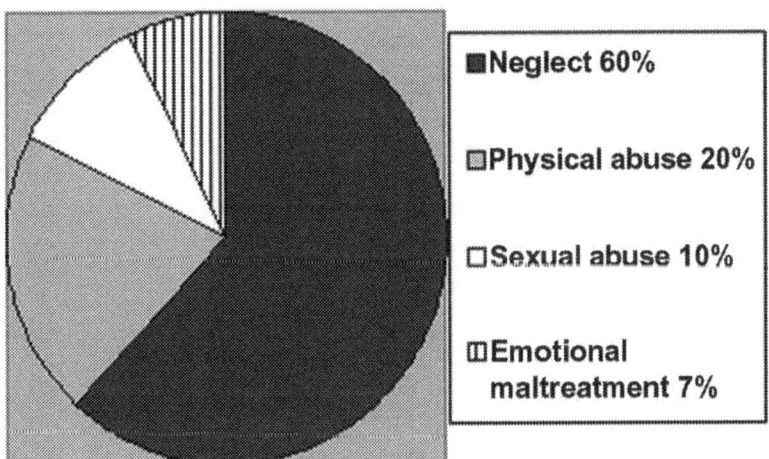

Here's what these numbers translate to for you: if you are a teacher in a school with 2,000 students, according to these statistics, *a minimum of 25 students in your school are the victims of child abuse or neglect.* So the odds are, you're interacting with an abused kid every day.

In order to protect these children from being the victims of child abuse and neglect, it is extremely important to report abuse to your local Child Protective Services (CPS) agency or to the police. In 2002, an estimated total of 2.6 million referrals concerning the welfare of approximately 4.5 million children were made to CPS agencies throughout the United States. More than one-half (56.5%) of all reports of alleged child abuse or neglect were made by professionals such as educators, law enforcement, legal personnel, social workers, health care providers, and child care providers. As you can see, it is people like you who are the frontline responders to child abuse and neglect and who make the majority of child abuse and neglect reports. So you play an important role in making child abuse and neglect reporting more acceptable and less taboo—and an important role in the welfare of children across the country!

The reason that reporting suspected or known child abuse and neglect is so important is because the most tragic consequences of child abuse or neglect are child fatalities.

- In 2002, an estimated 1,400 children died as a result of child abuse or neglect.

- Three-quarters (76%) of the children who were killed were younger than 4 years old; 12% were 4 to 7 years old; 6% were 8 to 11 years old; and 6% were 12 to 17 years old.

- One-third of these tragic child fatalities were attributed to neglect. Physical abuse and sexual abuse were also major contributors to the deaths of these children.

STATUS OF DOMESTIC VIOLENCE IN THE US[5]:

Domestic violence affects the children, too. Even if a child is not the direct recipient of abuse as parents or step-parents fight and abuse one another, the environment of domestic violence is still very damaging to children. Studies have shown that children who grow up in abusive homes have a high propensity to become involved in abusive relationships later in life as well. By getting involved now, you could play an integral part in protecting these children and breaking the cycle of abuse.

Here's a quick cross-section of domestic violence in the U.S.:

- In 2001, 691,710 individuals were victims of nonfatal domestic violence at the hands of intimate partners (their current or former spouses, boyfriends or girlfriends).

- Intimate partner violence made up 20% of all nonfatal violence against women age 12 or older in 2001, and 3% of all nonfatal violence against men.

- 1,247 women and 440 men were killed by an intimate partner in 2000.

- In recent years, 33% of female murder victims and 4% of male murder victims were killed by their intimate partner.

Children growing up in these homes can suffer trauma even if they are not the direct victims of the abuse. If you believe a child is suffering from trauma as a result of domestic violence, you may report it even though it is not legally considered child abuse in and of itself.

HOW ABUSE AFFECTS BRAIN DEVELOPMENT

How does trauma affect children? Take a look:

Travis was born the first child to a young couple in a small town. The pregnancy made Travis' dad very nervous, and even though he'd always been a bit aggressive, as the pregnancy progressed, he became physically abusive of Susie. Even though Susie hoped that the physical abuse would go away once Travis was born, it didn't. Although Travis was never hit by his father, he often heard his parents fighting. While he hid in the bedroom, he could hear his mom crying and could hear his dad slapping her.

Research now suggests that any exposure to violence or trauma in childhood, *even if it is not directed at a child,* alters normal brain development. This is startling news to most people who believe that children "won't remember" what is said to them when they are two years old, let alone what their two-year-old brain will recall about their mother yelling at their father. While children may not remember exact words or phrases, they become acutely able to recognize tone and emotion associated with fear, anger, and aggression.

Dr. Bruce Perry, MD, Ph.D., is a leading researcher in the field of child trauma and is the head of the ChildTrauma Academy. He has found that:

- the young brain is extremely sensitive to stress and develops differently in the presence of stress.

- exposure to unpredictable or chronic stress results in functional brain deficits and an increased vulnerability to future stressors.

- trauma directly influences the pattern, intensity, and type of sensory and emotional perception during child-hood [6, 7, 8, 9]

- any perceived threat activates a child's stress-response system in the brain; once this activation takes place, changes in brain development and chemistry also occur [10, 11]

The human brain develops and, once developed, changes in 'use-dependent' ways. Brain structures and systems that are used frequently or activated in a repetitive way can change permanently.[12], [13], [14] The more a particular brain structure is used, the more it will modify and 'build' in the ways associated with that activation. Dr. Perry has given two examples of how this occurs[15]:

> "The more someone practices the piano, the more the motor-vestibular neural systems involved in that behavior become 'ingrained.' The more someone is exposed to a second language, the more the neurobiological networks allowing that language to be perceived and spoken will modify."

Similarly, the more fear, anxiety, stress, and other threat-related neural systems are activated during young childhood, the more these reactions will become hard-wired into the brain. *This tells us that kids who are exposed to highly traumatic, violent, and stressful environments essentially become programmed to become violent themselves because they always live in a state of fear, anxiety, and stress.* Imagine the repercussions this can have on future generations.

The ability to respond to and control frustration, anger, aggression, and impulsivity are age-related. As the brain develops, our ability to control our own behavior increases. A young child may lack the ability to resist kicking or hitting when frustrated, but we would expect that a nine-year-old child would be able to resist doing this. However, if a child's brain does not develop normally because she has been exposed to trauma or violence, she may not be able to resist acting out inappropriately as she ages. Dr. Perry says that "any deprivation of optimal developmental experiences which leads to underdevelopment of cortical, sub-cortical and limbic areas [of the brain] will necessarily result in the persistence of primitive, immature behavioral reactivity and, predispose to violent behavior."[16]

From Dr. Perry's research, we can conclude that exposure to any type of trauma or violence, even if not primarily directed at a child, initiates a set of threat-responses in the developing brain, which will lead to over-stimulation of certain areas of the brain and alter the child's brain permanently. These changes and alterations in the brain may cause dramatic changes in the emotional, behavioral and cognitive functioning of the child. The specific changes in the brain's development and ability to function will depend upon the child's response to the threat, the nature of the threat, and a wide variety of other factors associated with the child, her family, and their community.[17] Therefore, we cannot say that "it doesn't matter" if a child hears his parents yelling, or that a child "won't remember" the stress of seeing her mother slapping her father. It does matter, the child will remember, and we must protect children from these life-altering observations.

SCOPE OF THE PROBLEM

In 2000, approximately 2 million reports of alleged child maltreatment, abuse, and neglect were reported by local child protective services agencies to the United States Department of Health and Human Services.[18] Of these 2 million child abuse reports, investigations revealed that 879,000 were found to support the claim of child maltreatment. Nearly 63% of the children were found to be victims of neglect, while approximately 20% suffered from physical abuse, and approximately 10% were the victims of sexual abuse.

This finding reflects a national rate of approximately 12.2 children per 1,000 children under the age of 18 who were found to be abused or neglected. *In a school or congregation of 3,000, this statistic would translate to approximately 37 children per year who are being abused.*

The 2000 Annual Report from the National Child Abuse and Neglect Data System (NCANDS) revealed that rates of reported child abuse increased in each year from 1990–1993, decreased from 1993 to 1999, and began to rise again in 1999. The rate of victimization was 13.4 per 1,000 children in 1990. The rate peaked at 15.3 children per 1,000 in 1993, and then decreased to 11.8 per 1,000 in 1999 before increasing slightly to 12.2 children per 1,000 in 2000.[19]

While this number may seem relatively low, *we must consider that numerous experts believe that most child abuse is never reported.* There are many reasons why child abuse is under-reported. Many people simply don't wish to be involved in abuse cases; they feel it is easier to not report and ignore the problem than it is to become involved. Another reason is that many people don't know how to recognize signs of abuse, or that may be confused about how to make a report and how it will affect them.

There are many factors related to abuse. Poverty, alcohol and drug use, mental illness, and post-traumatic stress disorder (PTSD) may contribute to abuse, *but do not cause abuse.* Abuse is about power and control; abusive behavior is absolutely a choice the abuser makes.

While abuse happens to children of families in all income levels, numerous research studies suggest that income level is strongly tied to abuse rates. Children from families with annual incomes below $15,000 per year have been found to be more than 25 times more likely than children from families with annual income above $30,000 to be harmed or endangered by abuse or neglect. Therefore, there is a clear connection between poverty and child abuse, but this does not mean that those who have limited incomes always abuse their children, nor does it indicate that if one's income level goes down, his likelihood of abusing his children will go up. What this means is that the factors associated with poverty, such as drug use, male joblessness, and mental illness, may also predispose someone to behave in abusive ways or lack the ability to differentiate between healthy and unhealthy behaviors.

For example, being a single parent and raising two children is a very stressful situation because all of the responsibility lies on one person's shoulders. If the single parent father were to be laid off from his job, his stress level would increase dramatically and the restraint he'd normally show under regular levels of stress would go down as his stress went up.

In addition to these factors that affect the abusers, three factors contribute to the likelihood that a child will be abused: a child's age, gender, and disability.

Children under the age of 4 are at high risk for being victims of abuse.

This is largely because these children are verbally unable to communicate that they are being abused and/or they do not know that abuse is not "normal" behavior. However, reports of child abuse increase with the age of the victim. This probably means that as a child gets older, the abuse is more likely to be reported. Our feeling is that abuse occurs to children of all ages, but that as children grow older, they make friends and develop relationships with other adults who show them that abuse is not normal. As they get older and are outside their homes more, they are more visible to people like you who can report the abuse. It is very hard to make an abuse allegation, let alone a report, so we believe it takes many years for a child to realize abuse is happening and then want to report. That's why it's adults like you who have the responsibility of getting help for this child.

Girls are at high risk for being victims of certain types of abuse.

Girls are more likely than boys to be the victims of sexual or psychological abuse. A review of data from 11 states in the U.S. revealed that 77% of sexual abuse victims were girls, compared to 23% who were boys. Victims of emotional mistreatment were also more likely to be female (53%) than male (47%). However, males were slightly more likely than females to be the victims of neglect, physical abuse, and medical neglect. This could either mean that girls are actually abused more frequently, or that they are more likely to report abuse. We think that abuse is under-reported by boys because there is so much societal pressure to "be a man," and that no young boy wants to acknowledge that he was taken advantage of by someone else and was "weak." Because of this, it is very important that we look for abuse warning signs in both boys and girls and act on any warning signs immediately. It's also important that we as adults do not assume that boys cannot be abused.

Disabled children are at a high risk for being abused.

Children with disabilities are abused 2–4 times more frequently than children without disabilities. Children with disabilities may be especially vulnerable to abuse because they may be unable to let other adults know what has happened to them. They may be unable to get away from abusers. Or, because of a child's disability, abusers may perceive him as being unable to communicate or get away, even if his disability doesn't prevent him from doing so. It's also important to understand that children with disabilities—even mental retardation—can feel emotional and physical pain as other children do, so we can't turn the other way and let them suffer in silence.[20]

What You Might See: A Typical Abuse Scenario

Melinda enjoyed teaching Sunday School and youth group, but she was always confused when she helped Cassie memorize Bible verses or do art projects. The other girls in the 7–9 age group chatted and made friends with each other, but Cassie, who didn't come to church often, didn't participate very much. She was in a wheelchair and Melinda thought she had a slight mental disability, although because Cassie's parents had never spoken to Melinda, she didn't know the nature of the disability. All she knew was that Cassie didn't interact with the other girls, needed a great deal of help and attention to do art projects, and even seemed surly sometimes. She never finished memorizing her Bible verses, either.

Cassie came to Sunday School one day with a purple T-shirt on with badly stretched-out sleeves. She kept tugging on the sleeves and Melinda finally asked her what was wrong, but Cassie said nothing and stared off into space. Bewildered, Melinda left Cassie alone and led the other girls in their songs. During the last song, she saw Cassie reach down and back to check the brake on her wheelchair. The part of her bicep that peeked below her purple sleeve when she did so revealed three long purple bruises, shaped like fingers. When the song was over, Melinda discreetly came over to Cassie. "Cassie? Are you okay? What happened to your arm?" she asked. Cassie just pulled the sleeve back over the bruise and looked away.

Discussion

⇒ Is Cassie mentally handicapped? *We can't assume that she is mentally handicapped based on this information. In fact, she is exhibiting withdrawal and isolation, signs of abuse.*

⇒ Do handicapped people feel pain as other people do? *Yes. Just because Cassie is quiet about what has happened to her doesn't mean she isn't in pain. This means she is even less likely to speak up for herself and will probably continue to be abused for many years if an adult doesn't report.*

⇒ Are children in church environments safe from abuse? *No. Children of all faiths are abused.*

⇒ Should Melinda try to talk to Cassie's parents now that she is aware of abuse? *No. Bruises in the shape of fingers are about as clear-cut an example of physical abuse as you will ever find. She should report what she knows immediately to CPS or law enforcement, and not to church administration.*

HOW EARLY INTERVENTION MINIMIZES DAMAGE TO DEVELOPING CHILDREN—AND WHAT YOU CAN DO

The best part is, early intervention really does help. We are fortunate to live in a time and a place where services for abused children are in every county, if not every city. Telephone hotlines are abundant and hospital care is widely available.

Early intervention is much more effective than late intervention. As shown by Dr. Bruce Perry of the ChildTrauma Academy, children who are removed from traumatic (including abusive) environments by age four have a much better chance of reassuming normal brain development. If they're not removed from abusive environments, their capacity for social skills— including empathy, compassion, and caring about others—can be severely limited.

More than half of abused children who have at least *one* consistently nurturing and supportive adult in their lives can escape the cycle of abuse.[21] This is because they are able to build some self-esteem with the adult's help and are made to feel valuable. Perhaps *you* can be that adult in a troubled child's life.

But what to do? Researchers from prestigious institutions such as Harvard and M.I.T. agree: create an emotional safe haven.[22] Let the child know you care and that what the child says, thinks, and feels is important to you.

There are some cases in which severely abused or neglected kids who have suffered profound cognitive (brain) development delays can improve, but only if adults work hard to create a loving and nurturing environment. Creating this loving environment is simpler than you might think.

Here are some basic ideas for creating a supportive environment. These tips can help kids whether or not they've been abused, but they do *not* take the place of intervention by Child Protective Services if a child's been abused. Always remember: if you suspect abuse, report.

Do...	Don't...
...hug a child who comes and leans on you (make sure to hug him appropriately).	...grab a child and hug him out of the blue, or interrupt his play to comfort him.
...listen and provide support when a child or teen brings up a troubling subject.	...dismiss the child or teen's feelings or try to change the subject to something more cheery.
...interact with kids and teens in their activities.	...routinely plop kids and teens in front of a TV or video, even if the material is age-appropriate.
...make available toys, games, books, and basic art materials that are age-appropriate.	...use broken or dirty toys, books, games, and art supplies.
...read an age-appropriate book out loud. (Reading aloud is good for older kids, too. Reading aloud builds important language skills that can help other areas of the brain to develop.)[23]	...eliminate children's and young adult literature in favor of books made into movies and TV shows.
...help teens develop their own thoughts and feelings about important issues by having frequent, two-way dialogues.	...tell teens "because I said so" without giving reasons why.
...ask kids questions and show them you care.	...minimize things that are important to them.
...validate their feelings, tell them you understand.	...tell them to "just get over it."
...pay attention to the child or teen.	...distance yourself emotionally.

Responding to an abused child of any age can make a difference, although the sooner a child receives help, the better.

Deliberately enriching a child's life using strategies such as those outlined above can help break the cycle of abuse from one generation to the next as each subsequent generation gains self-esteem and becomes healthier.

Just look at the effects of free lunch programs, Head Start, and others. These programs, with the help of funding, have met some of the basic needs children have. You don't have to start a big program like this, though—all you need to do is help the children you work with know that you care about them.

Another side effect: kids will love you!

Chapter Three

How Will I Know?

CHILD ABUSE WARNING SIGNS

How do we know if psychological abuse is occurring? If not all abuse is physical, can it be seen? What can we do, even if we're not sure it's abuse?

As we learned in Chapter 2, approximately 12.2 children per 1,000 children under the age of 18 were found to be abused or neglected in the United States in 2000. This is important to us because it means that if you have seen 500 kids in your teaching career, at least 6 were likely to have been the victims of child abuse or neglect. If you've worked with kids for many years and seen 5,000 kids, roughly 60 of those kids could have been abuse victims.

Christie, a local high school teacher, says, "I know I am a mandated reporter, but I'm not sure I can tell when a student is being abused." This sentiment was echoed by Mark, a Senior

Pastor at a church: "I've seen hundreds of kids and I don't know if they are just quiet and introverted or if there's something more going on."

Physical abuse is more obvious—kids will have bruises, trouble moving, or unexplained injuries—but in the case of psychological abuse, the injuries are less obvious. To know if it's psychological abuse, you need to look for a *pattern* of behavior. No one behavior or action means that a child has been psychologically abused. In general, abused children will have at least one, and possibly several, of the following warning signs:

Psychological Abuse Warning Signs for Young Children (Ages 0–5)

- Acts out violently and inappropriately

- Easily frustrated

- Refusal to cooperate with instructions, participate in group activities

- Withdrawal, has few or no friends

- Difficulty learning and paying attention

- Delayed verbal development, has difficulty understanding conversation

- Poor motor skills, appears to be uncoordinated

- Lack of bowel/bladder control, especially when new elements or people are introduced into an environment

- Difficulty sleeping

- Insecurity

- Anxiety

Psychological Abuse Warning Signs for School Aged Children (Ages 6–11)

- Poor grades

- Difficulty learning or paying attention
- Often categorized as ADHD or "difficult"
- Low self-esteem
- Aggressive behavior
- Hurts other kids or animals
- Sets fires
- Violent outbursts of anger
- Bullying
- Socially withdrawn, has few or no friends
- Poor social skills, does not seem to get along with peers
- Dependent, clingy
- Psychosomatic symptoms, (i.e. always has a headache, stomach ache)

Psychological Abuse Warning Signs for Older Children and Teens (Ages 12–18)

- Low self-esteem
- Anxiety
- Violent outbursts of anger
- Property destruction, vandalism
- Hurts other kids or animals
- Sets fires
- Reckless behavior and excessive risk-taking
- Unable to communicate verbally (i.e., the child can speak, but can't express herself)
- Alcohol/drug use

- Early sexual activity

- Bullying

- Social isolation, has few or no friends

- Development of inappropriate attachments (clingy)

- Engages in abusive dating relationships

Warning Signs of Neglect:

- Unkempt, poor hygiene

- Inappropriately dressed for the weather (shorts in winter, overcoat in summer)

- Unmet medical or dental needs, especially when the family has the means to provide good medical care

- Is routinely hungry and thirsty (more so than other children), reports not having breakfast and lunch

- Fatigue and lethargy

- Unusually thin, weak, or of poor muscle development

- Lack of basic intellectual and emotional skills

- Chapped lips and skin on a regular basis

- Left alone for long periods of time

Please note: Neglect is the most common form of child abuse. However, when playing hard, all young children become hungry, thirsty, and dirty, and then get tired, and that doesn't mean they are neglected. You should be looking for a pattern of symptoms or behavior that occur when a child is not properly cared for.

What You Might See: A Typical Neglect Scenario

Mr. Kastner had a boy in his 6th-grade science class who was a constant irritation: Ronnie never had his homework, came late to class, stole candy and peanuts from the prize box, and tracked more mud into the classroom on rainy days than other students because his pants were so long. Mr. Kastner knew baggy pants were in style, but Ronnie's clothes were ridiculous: if he didn't hitch up his waistband every few steps, they'd have fallen right off his skinny frame. It looked like he had on pants that would fit an adult.

Mr. Kastner realized something was wrong on a particularly stormy morning while he was helping Ronnie with a matching activity on new vocabulary. The class was learning about photosynthesis. As usual, Ronnie hadn't even started his work, and the class had been busy for fifteen minutes. When Mr. Kastner asked him what the problem was, Ronnie licked his chapped lips and said, "I don't get it."

The teacher felt his irritation rise as he leaned over Ronnie's desk to help. He put one hand on the desk and felt that it was wet, then saw that Ronnie's hair had dripped water onto the desk and his worksheet. "Where's your jacket?" he asked the boy. He wanted to add, "*Why can't you get it together?*" or "*If you don't study harder, you won't make it through high school.*" Ronnie just shrugged. "You didn't bring a jacket? It's forty degrees outside!" Ronnie shrugged again, and Mr. Kastner just tried to help him as best he could. He didn't want to embarrass the boy—the other kids didn't like him as it was. No sense giving them something else to tease him about.

Mr. Kastner ate lunch alone in his room that day so that he could get some papers corrected. While he was sitting alone in his quiet room, he realized that Ronnie had been exhibiting signs of neglect for some time, and the more he thought about it, the more sure he became. His irritation became concern instead. He put down his sandwich and went to the office to make a child abuse report.

Discussion

⇒ What symptoms of neglect does Ronnie exhibit? *Improper clothing, insufficient food, underweight, chapped lips, and a lack of basic intellectual and emotional skills.*

⇒ Why does Mr. Kastner feel fed up with Ronnie all the time? *It's not uncommon for teachers and caregivers to feel impatient with a student who doesn't progress no matter how much help they receive, or who seems to constantly have problems. If this happens to you, take a step back and reassess the situation. Does the child exhibit signs of abuse or neglect?*

If a child in your care exhibits several symptoms of abuse and/or neglect, it's time to be concerned. Many people think the best thing to do is call the child's parents and invite them in for a discussion, but if the child is being abused, this is one of the most destructive things to do. *Never* call a parent conference when you suspect abuse.

If a child is being abused, it's likely because his or her parents are unable to cope with their own anger and frustration. Your first instinct when you notice that a child might have problems may be to call the parents, but if the child has been abused, involving the parents could do the child more harm. Your calling a parent in for a conversation would create a situation that will probably make the parent feel angry, frustrated, and embarrassed. During such a conversation, both the child and the parent will likely deny any abuse, but when they get home, that child may suffer severe consequences for "causing" the parent to be called in for a conference. Abuse thrives in secrecy, and calling an abusive parent out could make him feel more threatened and increase abusive behavior. As such, talking to a child's parents is not appropriate if you suspect abuse.

Also, maintain safe boundaries. You should not launch a full-scale investigation and begin following the parents around with your digital camera. Your job is to be a look-out, not an investigator. Your county has an agency, Child Protective Services (CPS), whose sole job it is to investigate child abuse, so you should not try to do this job in their place. *Never* try to do any detective work to confirm your suspicions of abuse.

What you SHOULD do when you suspect abuse is call CPS. Just call them and talk about your concerns. Even if you're not sure, even if you're wrong, it's ok—they are there to help you and to protect children. The law does not require you to be right, it just requires you to be attentive and call CPS when you have a reasonable suspicion that abuse might be happening. As a matter of fact, you can call CPS and ask hypothetical questions or talk about abuse you suspect. If what you've seen does not constitute abuse, the agency will probably take no further action than to document your call. If nothing happens, don't be discouraged—creating a paper trail with CPS will help if someone else makes a report about children in that family.

Many people are reluctant to call CPS because they think, "I'm not sure that Connor is really being abused and I don't want the parents to get in trouble," or "I've heard about CPS! They just go out and rip kids out of homes and break up families." We can tell you that neither of these statements is true. When you call CPS, they will document your call and keep a record of the conversation; they will not immediately run out and arrest the parents unless the abuse is extremely severe. This is *very* rare. CPS strives to keep families together, not tear them apart, so don't be reluctant to call.

In other cases, CPS will investigate and will send an agent out to meet with the family. This again does not mean they will put the child in foster care the same day and cart the parents off to jail. CPS strives to keep families together by connecting them with county resources to help them, such as parenting classes, anger management classes, and the like. However, in cases of extreme abuse, the child may be removed from the home and in such cases, the agency is always acting in the best interest of the child. They are trained to recognize and investigate abuse— so you don't have to worry about taking on this responsibility. Your job is to just pay attention to the warning signs—when in doubt, call and make a report. If you're wrong, it's ok; if you're right and you don't make a report, the consequences could ultimately be fatal to the child.

TEEN DATING ABUSE WARNING SIGNS

Teen dating abuse is rampant in our society. A recent national study found that 8.8% of teens report that they had recently experienced some type of *physical* violence in a relationship (Centers for Disease Control, 1999).[24] Add to this the number of all types of non-physical abuse, the abuse that goes unreported, *and* the fact that most teens can't even accurately identify abuse, and you've got a great deal of our youth involved in abusive relationships.

Often, children who are abused by their caretakers go on to begin abusive romantic relationships in their teen years. Children who grow up in homes with domestic violence (abuse by or against one or both of their parents) may take on the behaviors they've seen at home. This is true for both boys and girls.

If you're a teacher, coach, or religious leader, you are probably more aware of dating abuse than parents are. Perhaps you've heard a guy call his girlfriend "bitch," a girl tell her boyfriend he's not a real man, or even seen a guy hit his girlfriend. If you're a parent, chances are you've probably not seen as much evidence of abusive behaviors, but you have an uncomfortable feeling that something's wrong. In any case, abuse worsens over time and draws much power from secrecy, so you can bet that *whatever* you've seen, it's the tip of the iceberg.

But if that's true, how can you tell when abuse has occurred? Below are warning signs of teen dating abuse. These red flags signal that a teen is, or might become, involved in an abusive relationship, either as the abuser *OR* the abused person.[*]

Warning Signs of Teen Dating Abuse

- Low self-esteem

- Anxiety

- Violent outbursts of anger

- Property destruction

- Reckless behavior

- Lying, sneaking around

- Controlling behaviors

- Trying to be perfect

- Cutting class

- Somatic complaints (headache, stomach aches, etc.)

- Inability to communicate verbally

- Development of inappropriate attachments (clingy)

- Alcohol/drug use

- Bullying

- Social isolation (spends less and less time with her own friends)

If you know a teen who exhibits one or more of these behaviors, they may need you to help them leave the relationship by contacting CPS. But most teens do *not* want to leave an abusive relationship. Many girls we've talked to say it's better to

---

[*] These warning signs can indicate that the teen is susceptible to a host of other serious problems, including suicide and depression. If you suspect a teen is depressed and/or suicidal, call CPS or law enforcement immediately!

have an abusive boyfriend than no boyfriend at all. So, your first goal is to gain the girl's trust and boost her self-esteem.

You can assist teens in abusive relationships by guiding them toward activities they do well and by praising them as individuals. Keep you eyes peeled for anything serious, including abuse, and report when you feel it's necessary.

Examples of Abuse

So just what does an abusive teen dating relationship look like? Below is a list of the types of abuse and some examples of each. Please note that these lists are not inclusive, and some behaviors may fall into more than one category. Also, keep in mind that homosexual relationships can also be abusive, and you should report that abuse just as you would report abuse in a heterosexual relationship.

Verbal	Emotional	Physical	Sexual
• Name calling • Insults and obscenities, includeing words like "stupid," "fat," "ugly," and "weak." • Screaming • Spreading rumors	• Mind games • Isolation from friends, family, and activities • Jealousy • Possessive-ness • Public humiliation	Hair pulling, restraining, pushing, kicking, hitting, slapping, biting, punching, assault with weapons, strangulation. Also, horseplay that "accidentally" gets out of hand and ends in injury.	Rape, including date rape, pressure to have sex or children, pressure to participate in forms of sex one person isn't comfort-able with, unwanted touching and kissing, exposure or obscene gestures, insults to a person's sexuality.

A Teen Wants to Talk to You—What Should You Do?

If either of the teens in an abusive relationship has confided in you, offer to talk and/or stay with him or her while making a report. If you suspect abuse and the teen doesn't want to help make the report, you must make a child abuse report yourself when a minor is involved. Have the phone numbers in an easy-to-access location. (Also, minors can request restraining orders, so bring up that option if the operator on the phone doesn't. A teen can get a restraining order against just about anyone who's putting them in danger, including family members, dating partners, neighbors, etc. See Chapter 6 for more information.)

You can help a teen who's troubled, and you should follow some basic guidelines while talking to teens about dating abuse.

How to Talk to Teens

- Give the teen time to tell his story. Don't offer advice or suggestions at first—just listen. As you begin to suspect abuse, comfort the teen, tell her you are there to help and part of your responsibility is to call for professional help (CPS) when you think someone is in danger. If the teen doesn't want to talk anymore, that's okay. If the teen suddenly begins talking in hypothetical terms, you should go along with the game if you're comfortable.

- Slow down. Don't pressure a teen to confess all if she isn't ready. People of all ages may have several conversations with a potential confidant before feeling comfortable enough to speak about abuse.

- It's not about you! When a teen ventures to talk to you, he'd probably like your undivided attention. Chances are, he's anxious and nervous, and has a lot on his mind, so sit back and listen, or you're going to jeopardize his chances of getting help. This means no manifestos on how things were in your day, no drawing examples from your own relationships, no insulting his music, TV shows, or style of dress. You are there to listen and guide.

- Report if necessary. You're the adult—do the right thing.

- Follow up. Arrange a time with the teen to chat again at a later date. Make the appointment before the conversation ends.

- Maintain safe boundaries. Although this may seem obvious to some, don't try to reunite the couple, don't try to talk to the other person in the relationship, don't go collecting evidence, don't bring parents into it, and certainly don't blab the information to other teens. For the young person who confided in you, any of these actions could be embarrassing at best and cause more, and more serious, abuse at worst.

You'll do fine.

What You Might See: A Typical Abuse Scenario

Laura, the head coach of the swim team, sat up front with the bus driver and made small talk. She thought it was unprofessional—and immature—for her assistant coach Nick to sit near the back of the bus with the athletes and hang out. But she didn't feel like there was anything she could say, since he wasn't doing anything wrong. Besides, she was nearly forty, and Nick, a semi-distinguished swimmer who had graduated from the local college, was about 26. She supposed he had more in common with the swimmers than he did with her.

They were on the way home from an all-conference invitational meet that they had placed first in overall, and Laura was happy with her team's hard work. Among the stars of the team was Cheryl Gray, a 15-year-old sophomore who had taken three firsts that day and anchored a second-place relay. She was already being solicited by two of the big state universities already and would probably be awarded a handsome scholarship. At the end of the day, Nick had led the team in a cheer for her and carried her on his shoulders to the bus, and now they all were reliving the day happily at the back of the bus.

By the time the bus pulled into the high school parking lot, Laura thought she would fall over with exhaustion. It had been a long hard day in the sun, and she was tired of listening to the bus driver talk about his bad back. She was ready to go home to her family and fall into bed.

First, though, she had to see all of the athletes off and make sure everyone left school grounds safely. They poured out of the bus and got into their own cars, or the cars of their waiting parents, and began pulling away. Cheryl Gray, her parka under one arm, handed Laura a handwritten note. "Here," she said. "Nick's driving me home."

"What?" Laura squinted to read the note in the fading daylight.

"My mom gave me permission. See you next week."

"Hang on a sec." Laura scanned the note, which said, "*I give my daughter Cheryl Gray permission to ride home with Nick Bell.*" It was signed and dated, and didn't look forged, but Laura suddenly felt uncomfortable. She wondered if they were dating. Nick and Cheryl stood a few feet away, waiting.

"Okay?" Cheryl asked. "Bye."

Laura hesitated, but Cheryl had followed the rules. A signed, dated note from a parent or guardian was all that was needed to ride home with someone else. Nick waved goodbye and unlocked his car for Cheryl, and Laura wished she could find a way to say no, but she didn't see one. She watched his taillights turn on and got into her own car.

The next morning, she had all but forgotten about the incident when her husband asked if she and their son wanted to go out to breakfast. At eight o'clock, she was sleepily pouring syrup over her waffle at the local pancake house, listening to her son plead for a puppy, when her husband said, "Hey, isn't that your assistant coach? Rick or Nick, whatever his name is?"

Laura looked up. With his swimmer's build, Nick was tall enough not to be missed among the crowd waiting to be seated. So was Cheryl Gray. He put his hand on the small of her back and guided her through the crowd to place their names, and Laura saw that Cheryl was wearing a frayed yellow sweatshirt with the hornet logo of the local college. It was Nick's sweatshirt; she'd seen him wear it to practice dozens of times.

"What's wrong?" her husband asked, as Laura looked down and put one hand on her forehead, under her bangs. "Why don't you go say hi?"

She looked at her son, who was happily dragging his sausage through the egg yolk on his plate, then met her husband's eyes again. "I'll tell you later," she said.

Discussion

⇒ Does Laura have enough information to report child abuse? *She suspects child sexual abuse, so yes.*

⇒ Is Laura responsible for child abuse because she allowed Cheryl to go home with Nick? *No. She followed her school's rules. It would have been better for her to call Cheryl's parents to verify their permission, and she should check the school's rules about student-coach contact. Laura should make a report.*

⇒ If Nick and Cheryl are not dating, can Laura be sued for reporting their relationship? *No. She is a mandated reporter who suspects child abuse and is making a report in good faith. She is protected by the law.*

LEGAL DEFINITIONS OF ABUSE

Now that you've read this far, you've learned quite a few things. You have learned that you're a mandated reporter of child abuse, you have learned some of the warning signs of child abuse, and you have learned that there are some serious legal consequences for not reporting abuse. However, you still may not be sure when you're supposed to make a child abuse report. In this section we will define the different types of abuse, and help you figure out what kind of behavior constitutes abuse and when to make a child abuse report.

Although the definitions of abuse may vary slightly from state to state, the Federal Child Abuse Prevention and Treatment Act (CAPTA), (42 U.S.C.A. §5106g), as amended by the Keeping Children and Families Safe Act of 2003, provides the following minimum definitions of child abuse and neglect for all of the U.S.:[25]

- Any recent act or failure to act on the part of a parent or caretaker which results in death, serious physical or emotional harm, sexual abuse or exploitation; or

- An act or failure to act which presents an imminent risk of serious harm.

So, CAPTA provides the minimum definitions of abuse, and each state provides its own definitions of abuse that comply with the minimum CAPTA standards.

For the most part, however, almost all states recognize and define four types of abuse:

(1) Neglect

(2) Physical Abuse

(3) Sexual Abuse

(4) Emotional Abuse

The National Clearinghouse on Child Abuse and Neglect Information provides some examples of these four types of abuse. The examples that they provide are only for general informational purposes because some states' definitions of child abuse and neglect will not include all of these examples, while other states will include additional definitions of child abuse and neglect that are not included within these examples. That being said, here are some examples of what generally constitutes neglect, physical abuse, sexual abuse, and emotional abuse.

(1) **Neglect** is the failure to provide for the basic needs of a child. It can take the following forms—physical, medical, educational, and emotional. Neglect occurs when a parent or caretaker:

- Physical:
  - ☐ fails to provide necessary food or shelter for a child
  - ☐ fails to provide appropriate supervision for a child
- Medical
  - ☐ fails to provide a child with necessary medical treatment
  - ☐ fails to provide a child with necessary mental health treatment
- Educational
  - ☐ fails to educate a child
  - ☐ fails to meet the special education needs of a child
- Emotional
  - ☐ does not pay attention to a child's emotional needs
  - ☐ fails to provide psychological care for a child
  - ☐ permits a child to use alcohol or other drugs

(2) **Physical Abuse**

- Physical injury (this includes minor bruises, severe fractures, and death) as a result of any of the following actions:

  ☐ Punching

  ☐ Beating

  ☐ Kicking

  ☐ Biting

  ☐ Shaking

  ☐ Throwing

  ☐ Stabbing

  ☐ Choking

  ☐ Hitting (this includes hitting with a hand, stick, strap, or other object)*

  ☐ Burning

  ☐ Otherwise harming a child

(3) **Sexual Abuse**

- Parent or caretaker does any of the following to a child:

  ☐ Fondling a child's genitals

  ☐ Penetration

---

* The exception to this is spanking. University of California, Berkley, psychologists Diana Baumrind, Ph.D., and Elizabeth Owens, Ph.D. presenting findings at APA's 2001 Annual Convention shows that occasional mild spanking does not harm a child's social and emotional development. Baumrind defined spanking as striking on the hands, buttocks or legs with an open hand, without inflicting physical injury and with the intention of modifying the child's behavior. For further information, please visit: http://www.apa.org/monitor/dec01/spanking. html

☐ Incest

☐ Rape

☐ Sodomy

☐ Indecent exposure

☐ Exploitation through:

- Prostitution

- Production of pornographic materials

(4) Emotional Abuse

- A pattern of behavior that damages a child's emotional development or sense of self-worth. This may include the following types of behaviors:

☐ Constant criticism

☐ Threats

☐ Rejection

☐ Withholding love, support, or guidance

- Emotional abuse is almost always present when other forms of abuse are identified.

These examples are quite extensive, but they are by no means comprehensive; depending on where you live they may be either under-inclusive or over-inclusive. So, the purpose of providing these definitions is simply to assist you in making a determination of when to report child abuse and neglect. When you have knowledge or reasonable suspicion of behaviors that fall within these definitions and examples, you should make a child abuse report to your local Child Protective Services agency or police department.

Now if you're feeling completely overwhelmed by these definitions, we have some good news for you—you don't have to know these definitions and examples by heart in order to make a report of child abuse. If you find yourself in a situation where you're just not sure whether you should make child abuse report, just remember these six words: *If you suspect abuse, then report.*

Chapter Four

How Can I Help Young Kids?

STRATEGIES AND ACTIVITIES YOU CAN USE TO HELP YOUNG
CHILDREN WHO MAY HAVE BEEN EXPOSED TO ABUSE

If you work with children who've been raised in unhealthy environments, you are likely to see a wide range of inappropriate behaviors that disrupt your group or class from working together cooperatively. If so, the good news is that there are several strategies and activities you can use to help minimize difficult behaviors and empower the student to make positive changes.

1. Modeling Appropriate Behavior

The first strategy is modeling appropriate behavior. Modeling simply means that you should behave the way you want your students to behave. If you arrive to class upset and irritated because the freeway was a disaster and the line at Starbucks was too long, you should still be kind to your peers and children. Children are often mirrors of their environment. If you act calmly and peacefully, so will they. So before you enter the classroom, try to relax, be calm, and focus on the positive aspects of your day.

2. Anger Management Techniques

It would not be a normal day in any group or classroom if someone wasn't upset about something. A child's parents may be going through a divorce, a child may have gone without breakfast, or a child's friend may have called him a name. Kids may have a wide variety of reasons for being frustrated, some more serious than others.

When you encounter an angry child, try helping the child to use one of the following anger management techniques:

Relaxation:

Objective: Children will relax through calm breathing.

Turn off or dim the lights. Speak slowly and calmly, and pause between sentences. Here is a sample script to help you guide your students through a relaxation exercise:

> *Okay everyone, we are going to do a special relaxation exercise now, so I'd like you all to stop talking, put your hands comfortably on your desk, and close your eyes.*
>
> *Now we will be completely silent except for the sound of my voice.*
>
> *I want you to take a deep breath in, hold it for three seconds and slowly let it out.*
>
> *Breathe in, breathe out......breathe in, breathe out.*

As you breathe out, I want you to think of the word "relax"

Say it slowly to yourself as your breathe out and feel your body relaxing...

Relaaaaaaaaaaaaaaaaaax

Relaaaaaaaaaaaaaaaaaaaax

Relaaaaaaaaaaaaaaaaaaaaaaaax

Now let's slowly open our eyes and have a moment of quiet before we start our next activity.

In our experience, it is best to try this activity several times—kids of all ages warm to it when they have done it once or twice already. The activity may be challenging for younger kids if they are too energetic to begin with and you may have to offer some type of reward for good behavior. Doing this with older kids can also be quite an adventure because as you know, silence in a group setting is a perfect opportunity for some students to make "creative" noises. When we did this with older kids, we would preface it with a statement like, "Because you are all so mature, I'd like to try an activity with you that I usually only do with adults, but I think you can handle it." Then suddenly, acting inappropriately doesn't seem so enticing anymore.

Pleasant Imagery:

Objective: Children will learn to relax by visualizing themselves in a calm, safe environment.

Turn off or dim the lights. Speak slowly and calmly, and pause between sentences. Here is a sample script to help you guide your students through an imagery exercise:

Here is a sample script to use with kids as you guide them through a pleasant imagery activity:

Ok everyone, we are going to do a special imagery exercise now, so I'd like you all to stop talking, put your hands comfortably on your desk, and close your eyes.

Now we will be completely silent except for the sound of my voice.

I want you to take a deep breath in, hold it for three seconds and slowly let it out.

Again, take a deep breath in. Hold it for three seconds...Now slowly let it out.

Take a deep breath in. Hold it for three seconds...Now slowly let it out.

Keep slowly breathing as I describe a place we are all going to imagine we're at.

We are at the beach on a warm summer day. The sun is shining and we are sitting on the sand.

The sun feels warm and good against our skin and a breeze comes by and gently washes over us.

As we sit on the sand, everything is calm and quiet and peaceful, we feel just like we want to drift off and fall asleep.

It's warm and calm and peaceful...

Peaceful...[Allow students to relax for 30–60 seconds.]

Now let's imagine ourselves slowly coming back to the classroom. Let's slowly open our eyes and get ready for our next activity.

Change Your Thinking:

Objective: Children will see the positive sides of frustrating situations.

When someone is really angry, she might curse and swear, or speak excitedly without thinking first. When a person is angry, her thoughts often become overly dramatic and more exaggerated than usual. She might think, "Ugh, this is the worst day of my life!" Then she starts to think about everything else and overreact to that as well.

Here are some examples of ways to help children change their thinking:

A Frustrated Child Says...	You Say...
"My pencil broke! I hate this. Bad things always happen to me!"	"That is certainly frustrating, and it happens to all of us. Would you like to go sharpen it, or would you like another pencil?"
"All the kids call me names. I hate them!"	"It sounds like it hurt your feelings when Liz and Cameron called you a bad word. But *I* know you are a great person. And look: you have lots of other friends in class."
"My girlfriend just dumped me. I hate my life!"	"You must be in a lot of pain. Let's talk after class."

Help the child realize that this momentary upset is not the end of the world and help him try to find another activity that he will be successful at. Or you can give the child a task to assist you and this will make the child feel both successful and appreciated. Help kids look for the things they can change instead of the things they can't change, and you'll be building their self-esteem while you're at it.

In a severe case, such as a teen being traumatized by a breakup, talk after class, support the student, and then connect them to other school resources (the nurse, a counselor) who can help. Then, remember to follow up with the student later.

Hot Thought:

Objective: Students analyze their anger and find what is truly bothering them about a situation.

When we're upset, it's often hard to think rationally about what's bothering us. One exercise that helps adults and children to evaluate their anger is the "hot thought" approach.

On a piece of paper, ask the child to write down what is bothering her. Then ask her, "What one thing or idea is really upsetting you the most?" Once that "hot thought" is identified, ask the child to write down evidence to support if the assumption is true, as well as evidence that shows it's not true. An example follows:

TEACHER	STUDENT RESPONSE
What's bothering you?	*I hate Suzy and Alex! They won't let me play with them.*
Why does that make you upset?	*Because I'm slow and I'm not good at sports.*
How do you know that?	*They didn't pick me to play kick-ball today. They never pick me!*
Are there some games whereother kids do pick you, or that you are really good at?	*Yeah, when I play soccer.*
So is it true? Are you slow?	*No.*
Do you get picked for soccer?	*Yeah, sometimes, but not always.*

So it seems like sometimes they choose you and sometimes they choose other people. Do you think that happens to most people?	Yeah.
So maybe it's not just you?	Yeah.
Well, let's try to find another activity that you can do right now.	Okay.

For older kids, you can actually have them go through an exercise where they write down evidence that proves or disproves their "hot thought."

Sample Evidence Page:

I am upset because: _____

My "hot thought" is: _____

Evidence that my hot thought is true:

_____

_____

_____

Evidence that my hot thought is not true:

_____

_____

_____

Conclusion: My hot thought is/is not true, and I should:

_____

_____

_____

It really does hurt a child when others are cruel. It's true that some kids don't pick to play with other kids because they're slow. It's true that not every child is the most popular child. You should not try to convince an unpopular child that he is really popular; rather be honest and gentle with the child and help them to understand that not everyone has the same skills, and build self-esteem by highlighting his positive attributes.

You might say:

Katie, not everybody in the world is a really fast runner and that's okay because some people are not meant to be runners. Look at some of the most important people in the world—can you think of someone who's really important?

(Allow the student to answer and guide them towards an appropriate selection if need be.)

That's right, the president is a really important person. Do you think he became so important because he's a good runner?

Right, probably not, so we all have things we're good at and things we're not so good at. Even me! Believe it or not, I'm not a good runner (or share some other relevant and appropriate story).

But I know you are really good at drawing. Do you remember how you drew a great picture of a tree last week, and everyone else started drawing trees, too?

With older children, vary the script to match their level of communication. We've used this technique with kids of all ages (and even some adults on occasion), so just remember the goal is to help them realize that no one is good at everything and everyone is good at something.

CONFLICT RESOLUTION SKILLS AND EXPRESSING ANGER CONSTRUCTIVELY

When conflict does occur, there are several steps that will help minimize the conflict and ensure everyone gets out of it with their self-esteem intact.

If both parties are very agitated, it's best to give everyone a cooling off period or time-out before continuing to talk.

Once both parties are less agitated, you can lead them through the following steps:

1. Each person needs to identify what the problem is:

   Who is responsible?

   What happened to make you upset?

   What really bothers you about what happened?

   What would you like to happen now?

2. The student should ask the other person if he is available to talk about the problem.

3. The hurt student should tell the offending person how he is feeling and why.

   For example: *I am feeling upset right now because you took my CD and broke it on purpose.*

4. The hurt student should allow the offending person to respond and listen carefully. The offending student should validate why the other student is upset.

   For example: *I didn't mean to break it, it was an accident, and I understand that I hurt your feelings.*

5. Discuss with the person different alternatives for resolving the conflict.

   For example:

   Student 1: *I'd like you to buy me a new CD.*

Student 2: *I can't, I don't have any money.*

Student 1: *Well, you broke it, you owe me a new CD.* (If this happens, the adults should stop the discussion and say, "John said that he doesn't have any money, so let's think about another possibility.")

Student 1: *How about if you trade me your other new CD for the one you broke?*

Student 2: *Okay, I can do that.*

6. If a resolution does not occur, have students continue to discuss calmly and look for mutually acceptable alternatives.

7. If the conflict cannot be resolved and the students are getting angry, interrupt the discussion and schedule a time for the students to come back and talk about it later.

By proceeding through these steps, students will have the opportunity to work out their feelings in a constructive way and to critically think about solutions. Helping students develop this skill is one of the most valuable gifts you can give them because it is one that adults often use every day of their professional lives. Also, if the child has never seen this modeled at home, you might be the one person to teach them this skill—a skill that could prevent them from behaving in verbally abusive ways in the future.

PROSOCIAL SKILLS

Prosocial skills are simply good social skills that include getting along with others, making friends, behaving appropriately in different situations, demonstrating tolerance, developing empathy, following rules, and many more. Because there are so many diverse skills included in the prosocial skill category, we've decided to focus on the two that are most critical to forming healthy relationships: demonstrating tolerance and developing empathy. If a student is judgmental, intolerant, and lacks empathy, the odds are very good that this kid will become abusive.

Demonstrating Tolerance

In order to be tolerant of others, you must believe in two things: (1) I am a valuable person who is not threatened by others, and (2) other people have value, even if they are not like me.

As such, helping a child become tolerant involves developing strength in each of these two areas. The first task is to build the child's self esteem and sense of value. Depending on the age of the child, there are numerous ways to build self-esteem. Here's an example:

Activity: About Me Book

Objective: Student builds self-esteem and develops self-knowledge.

Have each student create an "About Me" book or portfolio that contains the following sections:
-What I like to do
-What I am really good at
-The best things people have ever said to me
-My favorite things
-Why I am special and unique

Older students can create a collage, song, timeline, or map that shows important "uniqueness milestones."

Activity: My Life Timeline

This is an activity where students create a timeline of their lives and highlight important events and significant positive memories, along with a list of praise they've received along the way. The timeline can start at birth or at any point of their choosing. A sample appears below:

1990	1994	1995	1999
I was born, and my parents said I was an answer to their prayers.	We went on vacation to see the Grand Canyon.	I started school. My best friend is Chris.	I got an "A" on my science project. My grandpa said he was really proud of me!

Activity: Different Strokes

Objective: students realize that other people have value even if other people are very different from them.

One activity that works well for building tolerance in young kids is to have them first look around the room at everyone in the class and answer the following questions as a group:

-*Is everyone is this room the same, exactly the same? (If you have identical twins in your group, help people see the difference between them, too.)*

-*How are we different? (Age, ethnicity, hair color, eye color, etc. Help students focus on positive traits.)*

-*How are we the same? (We all need food, water, shelter, love, etc.)*

Then you can say, "So we all need many of the same things, since we have some things in common, maybe we even like to do some of the same things?"

"Let's look at some pictures of people who might be different from us and try to figure out what we could do together or talk about."

"This is a picture of Maria." (Hold up a picture of a young girl who has a special need—she might be handicapped or have a disability).

Explain that when Maria was young, she was in an accident and cannot walk, then ask: "what might we like to do with Maria?"

If you don't have or wish to use photos for this activity, you can substitute characters from different books that most students will know, characters from movies, or any other characters who are diverse that students will be familiar with.

Continue holding up pictures of children their own age or referring to characters who have different situations. Try to select images or characters who show diversity, including someone who is needy, someone who speaks a different language, someone who wears different clothing, someone who lives in a different country, and someone who attends a different type of religious organization.

Write the students' responses on the board as you go through the pictures and at the end, ask the students: "So what have we learned? Are we so different after all?"

Close with a quick summary and if possible, an appropriate story about how you have a friend who is different from you and how much you value that relationship. A story from your childhood would be more relevant than a story about yourself as an adult.

Diversity Appreciation

Objective: Older students recognize that diversity is a good thing and that people of all sizes, shapes, and sorts have had a great impact on our society.

Students research famous historical figures who've overcome great challenges and biases. You might give them a list of characters and ask them to write a script where the characters have a conversation, or have them prepare a 1-minute presentation for the group on how the characters overcame diversity and how these same strategies can be used today.

Developing Empathy

Helping students to develop empathy and to treat others kindly is one of the most valuable gifts you can give someone else. Empathy allows us to understand and relate to the feelings of others and act in ways that honors and protects the feelings of our friends, family, and new acquaintances. In our work with adults and children, we have consistently found that the most empathetic people achieve the greatest success and lead happier, more fulfilling lives. This may be because they attend to the needs of others and are likable people. Very few of us want to spend time or work with people who treat us poorly and regard us as unimportant.

To teach young children empathy, you need to walk them through how it feels to be treated poorly and what it means to treat someone with kindness.

How Does Larry Feel?

Objective: Children develop empathy.

Draw a picture of a child on the board. It doesn't have to be a fancy drawing—kids like to see you being imperfect.

Leave the face of the child expressionless, like so:

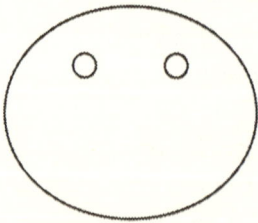

Then write several statements on the board that range from positive and affirming to negative and critical, like so:

Wow, you can really kick that ball far.
You smell funny.

Your parents drive a junky old car.
Come sit with me to eat lunch.
Can you help me with my puzzle?
I don't like you.

As you read each statement, ask the kids: So what kind of face should we draw on our person?

As they reply, draw the face on the cartoon on the board and then pause for discussion before going on to the next statement. Ask the kids if they have ever heard someone say something like that to them and if so, how it made them feel.

Repeat this for each expression and at the end of the lesson, close by saying, "We've talked a lot today about how what we say can make a big difference in how people feel, so the next time you're with someone, please say loving, nice things because we all know it feels so much better to be happy than sad."

Empathy Role-Playing

Objective: Older students role-play to build empathy.

Place students in groups of two or three and give them a scenario to play out. Perhaps it's a scene where two people are harassing a third to give them a homework assignment they can copy. Another scene might involve two students making fun of another student's clothes. A third scene might be two kids bullying the third into giving away their money or CDs. Have each group of three students act out three different scenes in which the hurt person is played each time by a different member of the group.

At the end of the exercise, write the following questions on the board and ask each student to write their responses individually on their own sheet of paper:

1. How did you feel about being the aggressor in one of the scenarios?

2. How did you feel about being the hurt person in one of the scenarios?

3. If you've been a hurt person in real life, how did you feel about yourself?

4. If you've been an aggressor in real life, how did you feel about yourself?

5. Do you think that people like to be known as a victim? Why or why not?

6. Do you think that people like to be known as an aggressor? Why or why not?

7. Think of some people you respect. How do they treat other people?

8. How do you want people to think of you?

Cycle of Poverty

Objective: Older students develop empathy by analyzing the cycle of poverty in the United States.

Students should respond to the following prompts:

- Describe how some people become homeless.

- Imagine a friend of yours was in this situation. How would it change your relationship?

- Describe how you think you'd feel about your friend and how that friend might feel about you.

- How would you feel if your family became homeless?

- How has learning about homelessness changed your feelings about people who are needy?

- How can you help people who are needy?

- What can society do to help people who are needy?

It's also wonderful if you can take students to see how less fortunate people live. Having students volunteer at a homeless shelter, soup kitchen, or children's home can help them see first-hand how difficult it is to be a victim of circumstances that are beyond one's control. This exercise will often help students to appreciate some of their circumstances in a new way.

If a field trip is not possible, students can read literature about the struggles of poverty and then discuss. Two useful titles are *The Grapes of Wrath* by John Steinbeck and *One Nation, Underprivileged* by Mark Robert Rank.

Putting it All Together

Many people act before they think, largely because we are biologically engineered to react quickly before we've critically analyzed a situation. But we now must make a concerted effort to slow ourselves down, calm down, think carefully, and then react. The activities above are designed to help you guide children through each of these steps and hopefully, to behave in more peaceful and productive ways.

HOW TO TALK TO YOUNG CHILDREN

Prevention

Ideally, you want to talk to kids about abuse *before* it happens to them. Whenever it is appropriate, you can talk to the small children in your care about sensitive issues. Be discreet, appropriate, and sensitive—do *NOT* show them what you mean (i.e., don't point to genitalia, don't use dolls, etc.).

Here are some things you can talk about [26], [27]:

- What kinds of touching are okay and what kinds are not. You can talk about physical abuse, such as hitting, and also sexual abuse. When speaking about sexual boundaries, be sure to be discreet. You can say something like, "It's wrong for someone to touch any part of your body that your swimsuit covers up." Talk about what kinds of hugs are good for us. *Always* give children freedom to say no to any kind of physical contact, even if it falls in the "okay" category. You can say something like, "You don't have to hug anybody you don't want to hug."

- Things people say that make us uncomfortable or sad, and things people say that make us feel good. Talk about insults and compliments and let kids talk about or draw how they would feel if such things were said to them. Let children practice saying "No" to such lures as, "If you come with me, I can get you an ice cream," "Can you walk to the park with me and help me find my lost dog?" and "Your mom said it is okay to come home with me." This is a great skill to practice in a class environment or with your own children.

- Talk about secrets that are okay and secrets that are not okay. For example, a new pet for your cousin's birthday is an okay secret to keep because adults know about it and because something good is going to happen to the birthday girl. A secret that is not okay to keep is any secret that adults don't know about, that makes you uncomfortable or scared, or that hurts someone else.

As we have said before, an important part of preventing a child from being abused is to build his or her self-esteem and healthy independence.[28] Here are some ways you can assist:[29]

- Noticing when a kid does something great and complimenting him.

- Allowing kids to talk about their opinions of books, movies, TV shows, whom they like and dislike, and why.

- Encouraging their healthy desire for privacy as it develops. For example, if a young child is having trouble in the bathroom, knock and ask how you can help, preserving their dignity as you do so. Don't barge in and say, "Oh, come on, I've seen it before," or, "We're all boys/girls here."

- Encourage the child in activities he excels at.

If a Child Seems Distressed

If a child seems distressed for *any* reason, and you do not have information that would lead you to suspect child abuse (in which case you would report without taking further action), you may try to talk to her.

Find an appropriate time and setting, and an activity that the two of you can do without stress. Preschool children can play with blocks or soft modeling dough, which can soothe them. You can also use puzzles or games. Let the child select the activity. Sit down with the child and participate in the activity by helping build the block tower or playing with your own lump of dough. Then you can gently ask a few questions, such as the following:

- "You seem awfully quiet today. Is anything wrong?"

- "Can you tell me what's bothering you?"

- "You're very important to me. You can always talk to me."

- "Did somebody hurt you?" (Only ask this if the dialogue or child's body language leads you to it.)

If a Child Discloses Abuse

If a child discloses abuse or anything else horrible that has happened to them, imagine how you would feel if you were telling this to someone else. You might feel embarrassed and afraid, and you might wonder if anyone would believe you. When a child discloses abuse or any other crime, you should do the following:

- *Report the situation immediately to the appropriate agency.* Tell the child that you must share the information with a few other people in order to help.

- Believe the child and tell him that he is not the only person who has talked to you about a problem like this.

- Listen empathetically.

- Soothe the child and let him know you will be there to help. You can say, "I know you feel bad, but this is not your fault. Sometimes bad things happen to good people. But *you* aren't the one who did anything wrong."

- Do not investigate further (in other words, don't follow anyone around with a camera).

- Do not tell the parents (or other abuser) that you are aware of the situation. A child could be abused further as a punishment for telling.

- Tell the child that he has done the right thing by telling you. Remind him that this is not the kind of secret anybody should keep, and that everyone sometimes needs other people to help them.

- Tell the child that if he thinks of anything else later on that he wants to tell you, you'll be there to listen.

Remember that the child's well-being is your top priority. Talk to kids about their boundaries, help them build self-esteem, create opportunities for them to talk about their concerns, and believe them when they tell you something's wrong. You can make a difference in someone's life!

What You Might See: A Typical Abuse Scenario

Erica Martinez was reaching for Mr. Allen's hand again, and his stomach dropped. "No, Erica, you're a big girl now. You can walk to the library on your own, in line like everybody else." He was a new teacher at this school, a recent transplant from the Midwest to a large inner-city Texas elementary school. The move, precipitated by his father's failing health, was doing him good. He enjoyed the time with his father, the chance for his own children to see different places, and the opportunity to practice his limited Spanish skills. The city was much more diverse than he remembered from growing up there. In fact, the school district was pushing for its employees, especially the teachers, to be culturally sensitive. Mr. Allen knew that they had been sued for racial discrimination the year before.

Erica got back in line with the other students. She was like glue: every time he turned around, she needed personal attention. Her shoes were untied, her lunch was missing, she wet her pants, she felt sick, and on and on. This was first grade, not preschool, for crying out loud.

It wasn't that he hadn't tried to help her. He'd written a note home to her parents, asking for a personal conference, but got no response. He wrote another note, this time in Spanish, but still nothing. Her parents were also no-shows on back-to-school night, even though the school had interpreters in every classroom and both the principal and his aide spoke Spanish.

At the library, the kids were supposed to spend fifteen minutes sitting and reading quietly, but Erica wouldn't sit down. "Please sit down," the librarian said, but she didn't.

"Erica," Mr. Allen said, "*Sit down.*"

Erica pulled out an orange plastic chair, put one knee on it, and leaned onto the table with her elbows. Mr. Allen walked over to her. "Erica, what's going on?" he asked quietly, kneeling down.

"It hurts," she said. "I got spanked."

"You don't want to sit down because you got spanked?" he asked, suddenly cautious.

"Yes," she said, reaching for his hand again.

"Who spanked you?" he asked.

"My dad. He spanked me again with his belt last night. He does that all the time when he gets mad."

"I see," Mr. Allen said, but he didn't know what to do. He knew that corporal punishment was more accepted in other cultures, and he didn't want to do anything—such as reporting the abuse—that might appear racist.

Discussion

⇒ What symptoms of child abuse does Erica exhibit? *Clingy, dependent behavior, psychosomatic symptoms (is always feeling sick), immature, regressive behavior such as wetting her pants.*

⇒ Is Mr. Allen right in believing she has been abused? *Yes. In addition to her other symptoms, she was whipped with a belt the night before so hard that it still hurts too much to sit down, and she tells Mr. Allen that this happens often.*

⇒ What's the difference between spanking and abuse? *This is a subject that many people disagree on. If a child has been spanked and you are concerned about it being abusive, make a report to CPS and let them determine whether this is abuse.*

⇒ Is it racist for Mr. Allen to report this abuse? *No. All children need to live in safe environments, regardless of their backgrounds. Abuse is illegal, regardless of cultural differences.*

PROFESSIONAL HELP AVAILABLE IN THE COMMUNITY— YOUNG KIDS

As you've probably read so far, there are lots of different things that you can do to help young children who live in abusive environments. When you take advantage of these strategies, there's no telling how powerful and positive an impact you can have on them. That being said, you may still be thinking, "I'm only one person. I have more students than I can count, and I don't even know how many of them are living in abusive environments. How can I possibly help all of them?"

We have some good news for you: you're not alone. There is help out there—professional help and community resources that exist solely for the purpose of providing you with assistance and helping those children who live in abusive environments. These community resources include the following:

Community Resources	When to call	Where to find Info
Child Protective Services (CPS)	To report abuse when you know or suspect a child is being abused	- Your county website - Call information - Yellow pages
Law Enforcement	To report abuse when you know or suspect a child is being abused	- Call 911 in an emergency - Call the operator - Yellow pages
Health Care Agency	For information about counseling and mental health services for children	- Your county website - Call information - Yellow pages
Shelters	When a child needs to get out of an abusive environment	- Internet (search for "youth shelters" in your county) - Call information - Yellow pages
Hospitals/Clinics	When a child has been injured and needs medical attention or assistance	- Your county website - Call information - Yellow pages

There are also some national organizations that you can contact for assistance in helping a child who lives in an abusive environment. They include the following:

National Resources	Phone #	Website	When to call:
Childhelp USA® National Child Abuse Hotline	1-800-4-A-CHILD® OR 1-800-422-4453	www.childhelp usa.org	When you suspect a child is being abused, or you need help
National Center for Missing & Exploited Children	1-800-843-5678	www.missing kids.org	When you have any information about a missing child
Prevent Child Abuse America	312-663-3520	www.prevent childabuse.org	When you want to know some things you can do to prevent child abuse

Helping children who live in abusive environments is a noble task, but it's not always easy. The great news is that you're not alone in your pursuits. There's plenty of help out there, and all you have to do is ask. So if you want to help a child living in an abusive environment, remember that you don't have to do it alone—help is just a phone call away.

Chapter Five

How Can I Help Teens?

A teen approaches you after class or another meeting and wants to talk. What should you do? Just listen, to begin.

While you listen, remember to withhold judgment. The most injured kid will probably come off with the most detachment, meaning she may act like the situation is no big deal. This is a defense mechanism. *In fact, the teen may even be aggressive or avoidant towards you.*

Next, there are three simple components to how you should behave when a distressed teen is speaking to you: you should monitor your physical, emotional, and intellectual responses.

Physical

Your body language expresses your concern and care. The way you hold yourself physically should reflect genuine care—don't just go through the motions.

As soon as you realize that the teen wants to be heard, reduce physical barriers to communication. For example, don't sit behind your desk or fold your arms; *do* sit to the side of your desk and at eye level with the teen. Give him or her your undivided attention-stop grading papers or putting away leftover soda. Make eye contact, nod, and pay attention. Avoid answering the phone. Focus all your attention on the student.

Emotional

Imagine how *you* would feel if you were telling someone in a position of authority about an embarrassing or delicate problem in your personal life. The teen who has sought you out is vulnerable and nervous, and probably very frightened, even if he doesn't seem that way. He has come to you because of a need to talk, so listen. If you start talking, the teen won't have a chance to, and you will be reaffirming your authority role, which won't make him feel like talking. You may feel like you know exactly what the problem is—the teen's new group of friends, say—but it's time to listen, not to offer opinions, advice, or criticism. Besides, you now know that warning signs of abuse can manifest themselves in all aspects of a teen's life, so a troublesome group of new friends may not be the root of the problem, after all.

Keep in mind that the teen may be testing you to see if you're trustworthy. It takes some people living with abuse weeks or months of tentative talking before they open up...if they ever do. You'll never gain someone's trust, and therefore won't be able to help, if the person doesn't feel they have permission to speak.

Intellectual

Remember that you are an adult, and you may be a mandated reporter at that. You know warning signs and contributing factors of abuse, and you know what can happen to an abused minor if the abuse is not reported.

If you see that the conversation is headed in a direction that will likely result in your suspecting or knowing of child abuse, pause the conversation. If you are a mandated reporter, tell the teen that you want to listen and help and that you may need to call for professional help if you're concerned about the student's safety. Tell the teen that if you know of or suspect abuse, you will have to let CPS know about it. Then let the teen decide if she wants to continue talking. It's important to inform her of your obligations or it will feel like you've tricked her and broken her trust if you make a report.

If a teen decides not to continue talking to you, that is not an automatic warning sign of abuse. Let the teen think over what you have said and leave if she would like. It's possible that with time, the teen will come back to continue the conversation. You can invite her to ask you questions if she isn't comfortable telling you much.

You aren't legally required to tell a student you're making a report, but in most situations it is morally and ethically better to tell him you have to report so that he won't feel as if you've tricked or betrayed him. If you learn of or suspect abuse, tell the teen that you're glad they came and told you about the situation. Affirm that they have done the right thing by approaching you, and tell them that the situation is not their fault in any way. Explain that you need to call some professionals (CPS) to get help for the student. Offer the teen the opportunity to participate in the report or listen in on the call. You can say, "After we are done making this call, I will be here to help and support you in any way I can." Even if the teen asks you not to report, report anyway; you are mandated to do it by law.

If at all possible, make arrangements with the teen to follow up at a later time. Before the teen leaves, remind him or her that talking to you was the right thing to do, and that you are glad he has come to you.

Dialogue tips for talking to teens:

- "I want to call people who can help you."

- "It sounds like this is a very difficult situation for you."

- "I'm glad you came and talked to me. You can come talk to me anytime."

- "It seems like this has been bothering you for awhile."

- "It sounds like you are really hurting."

- "I need to call people who can help you—do you want to make the phone call yourself? I'll be right here with you."

- "Why don't we talk again next week? Same time, same place?"

- "You've done the right thing by telling me about this. I know this must have taken a lot of strength."

PROFESSIONAL HELP AVAILABLE IN THE COMMUNITY—TEENS

As you have learned, there are lots of things that you can do to help the teens that you work with who live in abusive environments. By taking advantage of some of the strategies and activities recommended in this chapter, there's no telling how much of a positive impact you can have on the life of a teen.

That being said, there may be occasions where you encounter a teen or teens whom you don't feel you can help on your own. The good news for you is that you don't have to tackle it alone. There's no need for you to carry the whole world on your shoulders. There are plenty of resources out there—both local and national—that you can use to help teens who live in abusive environments. The truth is you have the power to improve teens' lives by connecting them with professional help that is available in the community.

Here are some local community resources you can contact to help a teen who lives in an abusive environment:

Local Resources	When to call	Where to find Info
Child Protective Services (CPS)	To report abuse when you know or suspect a teen is being abused	- Your county website - Calling information - Yellow pages
Law Enforcement	To report abuse when you know or suspect a teen is being abused	- Call 911 in an emergency - Calling the operator - Yellow pages
Health Care Agency	For information about counseling and mental health services for teens	- Your county website - Calling information - Yellow pages
Shelters	When a teen needs to get out of an abusive environment	- Internet (search for "youth shelters" in your county) - Calling information - Yellow pages
Hospitals/Clinics	When a teen has been injured and needs medical attention or assistance	- Your county website - Calling information - Yellow pages
Resources for your school/agency/ organization	When a teen needs to get out of an abusive environment	- School nurse, counselor, or psychologist - Crisis Response Team - Administration

If you're wondering whether or not you should call your local Child Protective Services (CPS) agency when the individual being abused is a teen, the answer is a resounding YES. When it comes to child abuse, the law defines anyone under the age of 18 as a child. So if you want to report that a teen is being abused, you can contact your local CPS or local law enforcement.

There are also some national resources that you can contact to help a teen who lives in an abusive environment:

National Resources	Phone #	Website	When to call:
Childhelp USA® National Child Abuse Hotline	1-800-4-A-CHILD® OR 1-800-422-4453	www.childhelp usa.org	When you suspect a teen is being abused, or you need help
National Center for Missing & Exploited Children	1-800-843-5678	www.missing kids.org	When you have any information about a missing teen
Prevent Child Abuse America	312-663-3520	www.prevent childabuse.org	When you want to know some things you can do to prevent child abuse
RAINN (Rape, Abuse, & Incest National Network)	1-800-656-HOPE	www.rainn.org	When a teen has been the victim of sexual assault

We applaud your efforts to help the teens that you work with who live in abusive environments. But we also realize that there's only so much one person can do. By taking advantage of the resources that are available both nationally and locally to help the children and teens you work with who live in abusive environments, you can make a powerful difference.

Chapter Six

When Do I Report?

IF YOU SUSPECT, REPORT

After learning about the many ways that you can help children and teens who live in abusive environments, you may be asking yourself "How do I know when to report abuse?" In this chapter, we will guide you in making that decision. As you may remember from Chapter 1, the standard for reporting abuse is as follows:[30]

Standard for making a mandated report
When you *suspect* that a child has been abused or neglected
OR when you *have reason to believe* that a child has been abused or neglected

That being said, a great rule of thumb to follow when reporting abuse is simply, *"If you suspect abuse, then report."* Even though this standard may vary slightly depending on the state you live in, you should report abuse when you either know or suspect child abuse or neglect. For more information on your state's reporting standards, see your state's child abuse and neglect statute, which is included in the Appendices of this book.

What You Might See: A Typical Abuse Scenario

Gloria wished she'd never started doing day care in her home. It was hard enough with the wear and tear on her home, the lack of privacy for her family, and all the paperwork for the state that she had to keep up with. Now, with the problems she was having with five-year-old Alex, she really wanted out. But she and her family were too dependent on her income for her to change jobs now.

Alex's mom was a single parent who used Gloria's day care five days a week, from 8:00 in the morning until 6:30 at night. He'd been coming to her for day care since he was two, and if Gloria added up the time he'd spent with her, it made his mom one of her best customers ever. It was people like her that made it possible for Gloria's family to pay the mortgage, buy a new truck, and even go fishing on the weekends. So when Alex began behaving badly, Gloria felt her stomach sink. She knew she'd be dealing with him all on her own, fifty hours a week.

First he began putting sand in the wading pool. Then he was pushing other kids. He kicked a four-year-old when he thought Gloria wasn't looking, and his name was featured most often by tattlers. He took toys out of other children's hands and stood in front of the TV screen when it was movie time. "Stupids!" he yelled at the audience of little faces that tried to see around him. "Babies! You're all a bunch of crying babies!" Putting him in time-out and taking away his treats didn't change a thing.

Over the next few weeks, his insults became more venomous, obscene even, and Gloria tried to speak to his mom when she came to pick him up.

"Alex, how could you be so stupid?" his mom had said when Gloria showed her the place on the backyard fence that Alex had ruined by driving a trike into it over and over again. Another day, when Alex tried to bite her, Gloria talked to his mother again.

"Dammit, Alex," his mother said, turning toward him. "I don't know what to do with you anymore!"

"I didn't do it—no, no, I didn't!" the boy whined.

"Shut up," his mother said, grabbing him roughly by the arm and pulling him toward the door. "Just get in the car. I'm sick of putting up with your crap." To Gloria she said, "Thank you. I'm sorry."

Gloria felt uncomfortable. She didn't like how Alex's mom talked to him, and she was afraid to tell her about any more of his bad behavior. It only seemed to end up with Alex's mom insulting the boy rather than disciplining him, and it never helped improve his behavior.

Gloria asked her husband if he thought Alex might be being abused at home, but he told her to mind her own business if she didn't want to lose customers. She also told her sister about the situation, but her sister said that if Alex didn't have any marks on him, she didn't think there was anything Gloria could do—she didn't have proof that he was being abused. So Gloria kept trying to deal with Alex, intervening when he bothered other kids and scolding him when he ruined toys or walked on the couch with his shoes, but she was at the end of her rope. She wished she had a co-worker to talk to, someone who could see first-hand what was going on, who might know what to do. She'd never felt so alone.

Discussion

⇒ Is Gloria a mandated reporter of child abuse? *Yes, because she provides child care.*

⇒ What warning signs of child abuse has she seen? *Alex has violent outbursts, does not get along with others, and refuses to cooperate and follow instructions. Also, Gloria has heard his mother verbally abuse him and grab him roughly by the arm.*

⇒ Other sensible adults think that Gloria should not report. What should she do? *She suspects child abuse, therefore she should report it. It can be easy to let others talk you out of reporting because it is such a hard thing to do, but when you feel something isn't right, call CPS and tell them what's going on.*

OVERCOMING BARRIERS TO REPORTING

Child abuse in any form is a scary, uncomfortable situation and one that you will probably wish you had never discovered. But once you suspect it, it's your ethical and legal duty to report it. Despite your knowledge of your duties and your understanding of what can happen to the child if you *don't* report, you may still have some of the following fears:

• <u>Fear of disciplinary action by a boss/supervisor who discourages reporting</u>. Unfortunately, some administrators discourage reporting child abuse. Some are under-informed about child abuse, others can be misinformed about CPS, and in private businesses, an administrator may discourage reporting if s/he is afraid it will be bad for business. If you feel your boss would be receptive to a conversation with you about child abuse, you can arrange for a meeting between the two of you. However, it's not your responsibility to do so; it's your responsibility to report. You cannot be fired for reporting. If you fear for your job, call your local bar association for free legal help. Also, remember that in the eyes of the law, reporting child abuse to your direct supervisor is never a substitute for reporting it to the proper authorities. You must make the report and not allow anyone else to do it for you.

- <u>Fear the child will hate you</u>. Some people are afraid they will lose the love of the child or teen if they report abuse. As an adult, your responsibility is the well-being of children in your care, not to be a kid's pal. A child, especially a teen, may be angry at you for reporting, but what would you prefer: a child in pain who thinks you're cool for a little while, or a child who is safer because you cared enough to report?

- <u>Fear the abusers will retaliate against you</u>. Under the law, you remain confidential as a mandated reporter of child abuse, and only authorities connected to the case can access the files to find out who made the initial report. If, however, you think it will be readily obvious to the abuser that you were the reporter, let CPS and law enforcement know your concerns when you make the report. This way, you will have a paper trail to back you up in case you should need it. Also, you can request a restraining order against the abuser if someone has threatened you. If a child is being abused by someone who would go so far as to threaten or actually retaliate against you, that child is in a very dangerous situation and needs you to report even more.

- <u>Fear the child will be retaliated against</u>. If you fear that the child will suffer further abuse for having confided in you, which resulted in a report, tell the authorities so when you make the report. Then, if you learn of or even suspect that further abuse has occurred, make a second report immediately. The child is in danger and needs immediate help. Sweeping the situation under the rug won't make it go away.

- <u>Fear that CPS will "rip the child out of the home</u>." We're not sure how the myth developed that CPS goes around snatching kids from their parents in the middle of the night for no reason, but so far, we have *never* heard of a case where this actually happened. In fact, conversations with lead agents at social services agencies reveal that CPS's goal is to help the child's family as much as possible in an effort *not* to remove a child from the home. Removal from the home is reserved for extreme cases in which CPS feels that no amount of resources or support to the family can help the child.

- <u>Fear that CPS won't respond</u>. We have, however, heard of cases in which CPS chose not to investigate a reported case of child abuse. A few distraught teachers have told us how they felt positive a child was being abused and reported the abuse, but saw that nothing was done to intervene. We asked the teachers how they handled the situation, and these honorable people told us that they persisted in their reports. "When CPS didn't respond, I called law enforcement, and vice versa," one teacher said. And they kept calling. A counselor told us, "I asked to speak with the person's supervisor, and that's how I finally got them to investigate." If you don't think the authorities have responded appropriately, stick to it and call again. The squeaky wheel gets the grease!

HELPING KIDS AND TEENS MAKE A REPORT

It's often helpful to invite the minor to participate in the report. Some children may feel empowered by participating, and some may feel reassured that they have some control over reporting the abuse exactly as they perceive it. When inviting a child to participate, you can say:

- "I have to report this to professionals who can help you. If you want, you can be the one to make the phone call."

- "I want to call and get help for you. If you want, you can talk to them also and let them know exactly what happened."

- "I know this was difficult for you. In order for me to help you, I have to share this information with some other people. Would you like to do the talking?"

While informing the child that you will have to report everything you know about the situation, be supportive and empathetic. This is very, very scary to a child who's trusted *you* with a secret.

If the child declines to participate, of course you should report anyway. If the child comes back after you have made the report and wants to participate in the reporting process after all, let that be okay: call the authorities back and add to the report. (The child may even wish to add more information.)

If the child participates in the report but leaves out key information, you can prompt the child by saying:

- "Was that all?"

- "Do you want to add anything else?"

But don't try to influence the report if you feel the child isn't being honest. You can always call the agency back later and add to the report if your interruptions and prompts are distressing the child and/or the report is incomplete.

After the child has finished making the report, you can say:

- "That seems like it was a pretty hard thing to do. I'm proud of you for speaking up."

- "That was very brave of you. It's okay if you are feeling sad."

- "I'm here for you. You can always come talk to me."

When and if authorities come to investigate, stay out of the way unless they ask to speak to you. Arrange a time for a follow-up meeting with the child before the child leaves.

What to Do at the Follow-Up Meeting

We've mentioned several times that you can invite a student to meet with you again after an initial conversation. But what should you do when the follow-up meeting comes?

First, your role should be to support the child or teen, not to gather evidence or offer advice. Show the child that you still care about him, even after you have learned something about him he might be ashamed of. Second, simply listen empathetically and be attentive as you were the first time the child spoke to you. If you learn of new information that constitutes child abuse, you will have to report it, but chances are the child is looking for validation for his trust in you.

Here are some dialogue tips you can use to start the conversation at the follow-up meeting. Once the child begins talking, remember to listen so that he has a chance to speak.

- "It's good to see you. How are you?"

- "I'm glad you're here. How have you been feeling?"

- "You look happy/sad/upset today. Do you want to tell me about it?"

Remember, there's no "goal" to this meeting other than letting the child know that he's important to you.

WHAT TO DISCLOSE TO THE FAMILY—WHAT TO SAY WHEN SOMEONE WANTS TO KNOW[†]

Now that you've decided to make a report, one of the most challenging issues to address is what you should tell the family

---

[†] In this section, we talk about confidentiality. If you are a psychologist, therapist, counselor, or social worker, you are bound to abide by different professional regulations and ethical guidelines, most of which will tell you that you should never break confidentiality. If you do not wish to break confidentiality, you should not admit to any of the above, and should simply say, "This is not an issue that I will discuss."

and friends of the child involved. Sometimes, when people want to stand up for what's right, they become vocal in an attempt to raise awareness about abuse that is happening right under other people's noses! However, there are many reasons why you should limit the number of people you disclose the abuse to. If a child has told you something in confidence, you may be one of the very few people this child trusts. Your turning around and telling others about the abuse could be hurtful to the child and may make her regret confiding in you in the first place.

Share the information only with people who really need to know. If you need to make a report, you should tell the child in an appropriate way and call Child Protective Services (CPS) immediately. You are not obligated to tell anyone other than the authorities—not even your principal or supervisor.

This is key: report to the authorities first; then it's your *option* to tell your supervisor. Some schools and religious organizations have crisis response teams and abuse reporting policies. Your organization may have a rule that says you have to let your supervisor know before you make a report. *While we applaud those organizations who have resources and protocol for helping abused and neglected children, you should know that you are NOT legally obligated to follow your institution's requirements for reporting abuse to your supervisors before reporting to the authorities, unless otherwise indicated by your state law.* However, you *are* legally required to report to the authorities. So if a school's policy of talking with your supervisor before making a report is making you think twice about reporting, make sure to follow the law and make a report.

It is also not required or recommended that you contact a child's parents if you are making an abuse report. In fact, it could result in the parent punishing or further abusing the child for disclosing the abuse. Do not call the parents if you suspect abuse or neglect. By doing so, you could place yourself and the child in danger.

After making the report, you do not need to tell anyone about the report or the abuse. However, the child's friends and family members may contact you and ask you to tell them what you know about the situation. *In this case, we think the best practice is to say as little as possible and pretend you have no information about the case (unless asked by a professional with a right to the information). Don't lie, but in general, the less information you give out, the better for the child.* It seems like it would be a good idea to let everyone know so that they can watch and protect the child, but more often than not, people get their own ideas about how they should "care" for the abused child and this care can be very destructive. For example, a person who feels very strongly about the situation may decide to confront the child's abusers, which could end in a fight or other traumatic situation that would be devastating for the child. The law grants you confidentiality for a reason, and if you do decide to tell someone you've made a report, you have waived that right.

Here are some suggestions on how to respond to the difficult questions your colleagues, the child's parents, or another student may ask you:

SCENARIO 1: Someone says to you, "Is it true that you called CPS and reported Maria's uncle?"

Your response to a colleague: "I spoke with Maria and decided that the situation needed some professional attention."

> This is an appropriate response for a colleague who may be concerned that if you didn't report, he should. In this case, you could elaborate if you feel it's appropriate. However, if you don't wish to share this with your colleague, you could say, "Thanks for your concern, but it's not something that needs talking about."

Your response to Maria's parent: "I'm concerned about Maria, is there anything I can do to help?"

> Here you are not answering the question dishonestly, but you are not alerting them to the abuse report. If a parent pushes you for a response and gets very

aggressive, you may wish to speak with your supervisor about the situation and seek their support. If you do not wish to involve your superiors, the best course of action may be to not respond at all and say, "I am not sure where you received this information, but if I did learn about abuse, by law I would have to report it." You could also say, "I am sorry, but I am not comfortable discussing this issue.'

Your response to another student: "I'm glad you are thinking about Maria, but there's nothing for you to worry about."

Kids don't need to know about the abuse or the report and there's nothing they can do about it. The best thing is for them to treat Maria normally because children who are victims of abuse already feel isolated and different, so singling them out or asking other kids to pay attention to them is not what they want or need.

SCENARIO 2: Someone says to you, "Jacob just told me that the police came to interview him because you reported abuse. What's going on?"

Your response to a colleague: "I did speak to Jacob and based on what he said, I called CPS."

If a child has told you and another colleague about the abuse, it's fine to tell the colleague that you did call CPS. However, if you decide to tell your colleague, realize that you are waiving your confidentiality as to being the one who made the abuse report. If you do not wish to do this, you might respond to your colleague, "If you are concerned that Jacob is being abused, you should call CPS." Again, you can always respond with, "I am sorry, I am not comfortable discussing this."

Your response to Jacob's parents: "Jacob and I did have a conversation about some of his concerns."

Do not lie to the parents, but you need not waive your confidentiality and tell them you made an abuse report if you do not want to. If you decide you do wish to tell the parents that you made the report, you might say, "Because of what Jacob shared with me, I was legally obligated to contact some professionals, but I know they will contact you to talk further about it if there's any reason to be concerned."

Your response to another student: "Jacob and I talked about some of the things he's been thinking about, so don't worry, everything is okay."

Again, the goal is to protect your and Jacob's confidentiality. If Jacob chooses to waive his and tell a friend, you don't necessarily have to respond. You may make the decision about whether or not you want to speak to the other student about the situation, but since the other student may not be in a position to help, telling him about a problem he can't fix will unfairly burden him.

SCENARIO 3: The parent of a child whose case you have reported says to you, "What are you? Crazy? I love my child, I would never hurt him!"

Your response to the parent: "I'm so glad to hear that you're concerned and I'm sorry you're upset. How can I help you?"

Here we assume that a parent is calling you and is very upset. In such a situation, it is best to try to calm the parent down, offer to be of help, and provide no information. If the parent pushes and insists that you explain why you made a report, you can respond in one of a few ways:

Or you can say, "I am not comfortable discussing this with you when you're so upset. If you'd like to come in and meet with me and the school/site administration, I'd be glad to."

Or, "I am not comfortable talking about this issue."

Or, "After my conversation with your child, I was legally obligated to make a report."

SCENARIO 4: An administrator says to you, "Those parents gave us a lot of money for our new building. How could you do this without talking to me?"

Your response to this administrator: "I'm sensitive to that issue, but based on what the child said, I legally had to make a report and out of concern for the child, I felt it was best to keep it confidential."

> It's hard to fight with this response. Regardless of what someone may have given to your institution, child abuse is against the law and must be reported. You have a legal duty to report the abuse, not to your administrator, but to CPS. You followed the law and your decision to protect the child's privacy is one that should be respected. If the administrator asks why you couldn't trust them to protect the child's privacy, you might offer that the child asked you not to tell anyone or that you only told the child you'd tell CPS.

SCENARIO 5: The child's parent says to you, "I can't believe you'd do this. I'm going to sue you!"

Your response to the parent: "I'm really sorry you're upset. I made a report based on my legal obligations. CPS and I want to make sure that every child is protected, so based on what I heard, I had to contact the authorities. I hope that they will be of help to your family."

> Legally, you can't be sued for reporting if you did so in good faith. If you are nervous about this, you can speak with your administrators, supervisors, union represen-

tative, or legal representative. By providing the response above, you are admitting that you made the report, so be cautious. If the parent doesn't know you made the report, you might not want to volunteer this information. In such a case, just say, "I am sorry you are upset. If I did know of or suspect child abuse, I am required by law to report it."

Remember: less is more! The less you say about the abuse and the report, the better for you and the child involved. Making a report is not easy, but neither is talking to an adult when you are a frightened child. Please treat a child who reports to you with great respect and concern by only sharing his or her story with the proper authorities.

Throughout this section we have talked about confidentiality. If you are a psychologist, therapist, counselor, or social worker, you are bound to abide by different professional regulations and ethical guidelines, most of which will tell you that you should never break confidentiality. If you do not wish to break confidentiality, you should not admit to any of the above, and should simply say, "This is not an issue that I will discuss."

WHY GETTING IN THE MIDDLE CAN BE DANGEROUS

In the last section we talked about how to respond to difficult situations that may arise after you've made an abuse report. As you read through that section, you might have thought: *"Why is it really such a big deal not to tell the parents? It's their kid—they have a right to know!"*

Many of us may also think that if it was our child, we'd want to know about the abuse allegations, but there are two very good reasons why you should not tell the parents: *it can be dangerous for you and it can be dangerous for the child.*

If abuse is taking place and you call a child's parents, you have added embarrassment, anger, and frustration to a situation that a parent already struggles with. If someone is abusing their child, it is likely they have a difficult time coping with anger and frustration, have limited parenting skills, and have limited impulse control. If you contact this parent and tell them you suspect abuse, they may become upset and take this anger out on the child, their spouse, the family pet, or even you.

Most abusive parents lack the ability to step back from the situation and take your call as a sign that it is time to get help. If they had this ability, they probably would have already sought help. If abuse has escalated into physical abuse or if psychological abuse is happening on an ongoing basis, it's not going to get better without professional help. *As such, you should never contact a parent in lieu of making a report to CPS.*

You might also be inclined to call the child's non-abusive parent, grandparents, friends, or family friends. Some mandated reporters hope that these people will protect and support the abused child, but again, this may not work out. Family members and friends may feel you have over-stepped your boundaries by butting in on a personal "family matter." They may react very aggressively towards you or worse, may act aggressively towards the child. After all, they care about the abuser as well, so they may want to protect that person, too. In addition, *you* have the legal duty to report; not the parents or grandparents.

Most abusers learn to be abusive by being abused themselves. It is possible that if a child is being abused by her father, the father may have also been abused by his father. This is just an example, but if it was true and you called the child's grandfather, he might respond by verbally berating the father who would then respond by abusing the child even more. The family is likely to be protective of the abuser and the abused child, so your interacting with them will complicate the situation and make it worse for the child.

As for speaking with family friends, the PTA, the bus driver, or anyone else, there's really no good reason to do this. Even though your intentions may be good, the probable outcome is that the child will endure more pain, discomfort, and embarrassment every time their story is shared with another person or they are singled out for special treatment. *The only call you should make to report abuse is to Child Protective Services or local law enforcement, such as the police.*

Chapter Seven

What Happens Now That I Have Decided to Report?

Next steps: How to report child abuse

Let's walk through the reporting process. In this section, you will find instructions on how to make child abuse report.

- In the case of an emergency (i.e. the child's life is in danger), the first thing you should do is call 911.

In a non-emergency situation (i.e., the child's life is *not* in danger), you should call your local Child Protective Services (CPS) agency or local law enforcement to report the abuse. If you do not know the phone number for your local CPS agency, here are a few ways that you can find it:

- Call information (411) and ask for the number of your local CPS agency.

- Look up "Child Protective Services" in the Yellow pages.

- Do an internet search using a search engine (such as Google) and type in the county and state that you live in and the words "child protective services." For example, if you live in Orange County, California, you would type in "Orange County California child protective services." This search will bring up the county's web page which will contain a link to CPS.

- Call local law enforcement.

If you want to report suspected child abuse in a state other than the one in which you live or you do not have access to any of the resources above to help you find your local CPS agency, you can call this national hotline:

Childhelp USA® National Child Abuse Hotline
1-800-4-A-CHILD®
(1-800-422-4453)
TDD: 1-800-2-A-CHILD

Childhelp USA® is a nonprofit organization that can provide you with local reporting numbers and the organization also has hotline counselors that can provide you with referrals.

Once you have made the call to report abuse, you may also have to file some additional paperwork for the child abuse report to be made complete. Your local CPS agency should provide you with guidance on how to proceed if a written report is required. If they do not ask for a written report, do not assume that one is not required. Feel free to go ahead and ask if they also need you to fill out a written report, and ask where you can find the required forms.

If you're a teacher or a counselor in a school, your administration should have child abuse report forms on file. If you work with children in some other capacity, depending on where you work, you may or may not have ready access to these forms. In that case, you can acquire the necessary forms in one of two ways: 1) you should be able to download child abuse report forms from your local CPS agency website 2) you can call CPS to request a faxed version of the form.

If child abuse report forms are available online in your county, you can find these forms by doing an internet search similar to the one listed above. Using a search engine (like Yahoo!), type in your county, state, and the words "child abuse report form." For example if you live in Orange County, California, you would type in "Orange County California child abuse report form." This search should return a website from which you can download the child abuse report form.

As you can see, the process of making a child abuse report is easy—all you need to do is call and fill out some paperwork if CPS requires it. Think about it this way: making the decision to report child abuse is probably the hardest part of this process, but once you make the decision, the rest is easy, and you could be playing a pivotal role in saving the life of a child.

THE ROLE OF CPS

Now that you know how to make a child abuse report, you may be wondering what Child Protective Services (CPS) does once a report is made. To begin, here's what CPS does *not* do. Contrary to popular belief, CPS is not some malevolent government agency that goes around ripping children out of their homes. CPS does not remove children from their homes without *very* good reason. The main goal of CPS is to promote the well-being of children by ensuring safety, achieving family stability, and strengthening families to successfully care for their children.[31]

Here's what CPS *does* do: When you make a report of child abuse, your local CPS agency receives the report and then evaluates it. If the report meets your state's criteria for defining a potential child abuse incident, then it is assigned to a CPS case worker. Once it is assigned, CPS will review the report and determine if an investigation is necessary. *However, not all reports of abuse will result in an investigation.* The purpose of the investigation is to determine whether the incident of child abuse occurred. If CPS discovers that an incident of child abuse occurred, the name of the person who committed the abuse is placed on a central registry. After all of this takes place, depending on the situation, families may receive support services, and a child will only be removed from the home if the situation absolutely warrants a child's removal.

So if you're feeling hesitant about reporting, rest assured that making a report of child abuse does not mean that you're placing a child in jeopardy of being removed from their home. CPS does their best to help keep the family together and support the family by linking them to agencies that can help. CPS will only remove a child if they determine that it is in the best interests of the child. So remember, *"If you suspect abuse, then report."*

THE ROLE OF LAW ENFORCEMENT

CPS and your local law enforcement agency should cross-report to each other. In other words, reports received at one agency that are relevant to the other should be shared.

RESTRAINING ORDERS

After making a report of abuse, you may want to know what other resources are available to help a child or teen that is living with abuse. Depending on where you live, children or teens living with abuse may be eligible for a restraining order.

A restraining order is a legal order that a court can issue to require one person to stay away from another person. Sometimes a restraining order is also referred to as a protective order, protection order, emergency restraining order (ERO), temporary restraining order (TRO), temporary protection order (TPO), or some other name similar to these.[32] Restraining order laws are state laws and not federal laws. Therefore, each state will have a different restraining order law. Restraining orders can usually be obtained by filling out the appropriate paperwork with the local court clerk.

The good news for children is that they may be eligible for a restraining order against their abuser because many states will allow the court to make decisions regarding the care and safety of children. A state court can issue a restraining order, and order an abuser to stay away from a child and have no contact with the child's doctors, daycare, school, or after-school job.

Courts may also issue restraining orders for teens ordering their boyfriend or girlfriend to stay away from them. The restraining order could also prohibit the teen's boyfriend or girlfriend from seeing or contacting them. Once again, each state has a different law regarding restraining orders, and not all states allow individuals under 18 years of age to obtain a restraining order. However, if they are available in your state, they can be a powerful tool to help stop abuse.

HOW TO SUPPORT SOMEONE DURING THE REPORTING PROCESS

You know that reporting child abuse (or teen relationship abuse) can be a sticky situation, or you wouldn't have picked up this book. It can be especially so for the people who are directly involved. Once a report has been filed, you can still offer emotional support in the following ways:

Invite the abused child to participate in the report. As we've said before, this can empower the child and give him a little control over his life, which may not happen often.

If someone has confided in you, arrange a follow-up meeting. Remember, arrange a time to follow up with the child or teen so that she can talk about any new concerns. Remind her that she has done the right thing by reaching out.

Lend an ear. The abused child or student will probably have a lot of inner turmoil and anxiety to process. You can help by lending an ear, and you don't have to give advice or offer solutions (of course, if you learn of abuse or another crime, you may have to make a follow-up call to the authorities). Just talking can help a person relax and feel better.

Suggest resources. At a minimum, your local area most likely has a police station and a hospital, both of which should be equipped to handle child abuse, rape, and other crises. If you live in a densely-populated area or are just plain fortunate, you may have access to runaway shelters, drug treatment facilities, and counseling, all of which you can suggest to someone in crisis. When all else fails, some of the toll free numbers at the back of this book can be accessed from any place in the U.S. A brief internet search can also yield other resources in your area. To be prepared, type up a list of pertinent local phone numbers and keep copies of the list in a highly-visible area where concerned children, teens, and adults can access them *without* having to ask.

Comply with the authorities. Don't do any investigating of your own, and don't get involved in an investigation unless the police or CPS ask you to do so. You could jeopardize the safety of the child and the efficiency of the investigation.

Re-report as needed. As you have read, there are some cases in which CPS does not determine that an investigation is necessary. However, if you are convinced that a child is in danger, call again. Be a pest if you have to. If you're still not getting the response you want, ask to speak with the supervisors at the agency you have contacted. If that doesn't work, call another agency. Keep calling until you get the response you want!

Last, but not least...Get some relief for *yourself.* We know how hard reporting child abuse can be. Depending on the severity of the abuse you have learned of, or the frequency with which you have to report it, you may need to relieve some of your own emotional stress. If you can, a session or two with a counselor can help you through the stress of dealing with child abuse. There's no shame in getting professional help, and relieving emotional stress is a very common need. A counselor or therapist will probably identify with you because they understand mandated reporting laws and will know exactly what you're going through. (Counselors and therapists are mandated reporters, too.)

And it never hurts to take an emotional break by engaging in another activity, such as playing with your own kids, practicing a sport, visiting with friends, or turning to your faith. In any event, monitor yourself for signs of mild depression or anxiety and make a point of staying active and engaged in the rest of your life. You will have nothing to give the children in your life if you don't take care of yourself first.

HOW TO HANDLE THE GUILT AND ANXIETY YOU FEEL ABOUT REPORTING

Now that you've made your report to CPS, there are probably a million questions running through your mind, such as:

Did I do the right thing?

What if I'm wrong?

What if they take the child out of the home?

What if the parents sue me?

What if I get fired?

Let's go through these concerns one by one.

Did I do the right thing? If you are concerned about whether or not you did the right thing, ask yourself: did you have a reasonable suspicion that abuse was happening? If yes, then you absolutely did the right thing by reporting! Maybe you are not sure that your suspicion was reasonable. Reasonableness is defined in the law as objectively reasonable, which means that if a reasonable person in your position would feel the same way about a situation, your suspicion is reasonable. Furthermore, you've probably worked with many children and have a strong instinct for situations where something's not quite right. It's a good idea to trust your instincts. If it turns out that you were wrong, that's okay, because you reported in good faith. It's better to be wrong and have done the right thing, than to have been right and done nothing.

What if I'm wrong? If you were wrong, you will be protected by the law, as long as you honestly felt that abuse might have been occurring. If a parent, peer, or school official confronts you about this issue and says, "How could you have called CPS? The child wasn't being abused!" All you need to say is, "I was trying to protect the child and I thought reporting was the right thing to do." It's okay to be wrong if you were acting in the best interests of the child.

What if they take the child out of the home? If an investigation is done and a child is removed from the home, it is for a very severe reason and you should feel very good about having done the right thing by calling CPS. Remember that CPS rarely removes children from homes unless the abuse is extreme and/or can be verified. So if a child is removed, it is because she is in extreme danger. It's likely you saved the child's life and we commend you! It's important to remember that the goal of CPS is not to rip children out of their homes, but rather to provide the family with the help, guidance, and resources they need to stay together in a healthy way.

What if the parents sue me? In a society as litigious as ours, it's natural for you to be concerned that the parents might try to sue you, whether or not the abuse report turns out to be true. In almost every state, there are laws that prevent you from being sued by a parent or guardian if you made an honest report of possible abuse based on reasonable suspicions. However, if you made the report out of spite because you were angry at the parents for being difficult, making a report would be unethical and you could be sued. And remember, you could be sued for failure to report. So it is very important that when you do suspect abuse, you report it immediately.

What if I get fired? It is also against the law for a school to terminate your employment for reporting abuse. If you are a mandated reporter, it is a state and federal law that you must report suspected child abuse; failure to do so would be breaking the law. If your boss were to threaten or intimidate you into not filing a report, they would be committing a crime by telling you to break the law. This practice is illegal and you should still make the child abuse report.

You might also have anxiety about what will happen to the child if they are removed from the home and how this will affect the child in the long run. If you reported abuse and a child was removed from his home, rest assured that professionals who are trained to help, and who have the very best interests of the child at heart, are working to make that child's life better. You cannot take on the responsibility of protecting a child for the rest of his life—that job is assigned to law enforcement and social service agents. The most loving thing you can do for a child is to make a report and let the system work to place that child in a safer environment.

Once you make a report, you may never know what the outcome of the case is. CPS may or may not tell you. You simply need to trust that what you did was the right thing because you acted in the best interest of the child.

If you still find yourself concerned about a child who you know was taken into protective custody, feel free to contact the child's social worker. If it is possible and if it is in the best interest of the child, you may be able to remain in contact with the child. The child may greatly benefit from knowing that you care about her well being and are committed to seeing her get the help she needs. This may not always be possible, but if you'd like to, talk to the child's social worker and ask how or if you can be included in the child's life.

All of the questions, concerns, and worries you have after making a report of abuse are normal and understandable. It is important for you to know that many people who make a child abuse report feel exactly the way you do now. But focus on the fact that you took action to improve the life of a child and that without your efforts, that child might have suffered in silence for a very long time. *Your actions make you a hero.*

WHY DOING THE HARD THING IS THE RIGHT THING

For 8-year-old Bryan, this morning was like any other. His mom had already left for work when his alarm awoke him at 6 a.m. He got up and started getting ready for school. He looked for fresh clothes, but there weren't any, so he put on some mildly worn jeans, socks, and a T-shirt from the hamper.

Bryan rushed to the kitchen to make a quick lunch before catching the bus to school. The fridge was empty except for a loaf of bread, a jar of pickles, and a carton of milk that had been there for a couple of weeks. He grabbed a piece of bread and his backpack and ran out the door, forgetting all about the incomplete math homework on the kitchen table.

His ride to school was a lonely one. He didn't really have many friends—after all, who wanted to sit next to the smelly kid? He walked up the steps, through the gate, and into his third-grade classroom, taking his seat near the back of the room. When Bryan started to take out his binder, he realized he had left his homework at home. Today would not be a good day. He was sure that Ms. Malone would put his name on the board.

Sure enough, when his teacher saw that his homework was missing, she wrote his name on the board and asked him to stay after class. Bryan felt even worse when he saw the looks of his classmates and heard one of them whisper that he was stupid. Bryan knew that was probably true because he heard that a lot at home, too.

He stayed after school to serve detention and arrived home later than usual. His mom was furious: his room had not been cleaned, he had not done any laundry, and he had not started to make dinner like she'd taught him. She shouted at Bryan, "You're a loser, just like your dad! He never could do anything right, and neither can you!"

When he explained that he had to stay late at school for not turning in his homework, she got even more upset. "As hard as I work, as much as I try to teach you, you just won't learn! Go to your room. If you don't have dinner tonight, maybe next time you'll remember to do your homework." Bryan walked to his room, closed the door, and turned on the TV. He lay down on his bed and waited for the next day, wondering when things would get better.

In thinking about Bryan and the thousands of children who experience neglect and abuse every day, we ask you: if you won't help this child, who will? All of us will encounter a Bryan in our lives. You do have the strength and the knowledge to help. Please answer their calls for help—speak up and save a life.

Appendices

APPENDIX

APPENDIX I

Training Your Staff and Forming Organizational Response Plans

If you are in a supervisory position, there are a number of things you can do to help your staff understand their mandated reporting duties and facilitate your organization's response to abuse.

During training, be sure to cover, at a minimum, the following topics:

- The definitions of child abuse and teen relationship abuse.

- The warning signs of child abuse and teen relationship abuse.

- The legal obligations of your staff.

- The phone or fax numbers for reporting abuse in your area. Provide copies of your area's fax report forms, if available.

- Your support for staff who fulfill their duties. This is especially important—no one will want to report child abuse or discuss problems with you if they fear for their job.

- Encourage your staff to freely call CPS with inquiries and remind them that they don't have to have proof of abuse to call.

- Co-create an organizational response plan. Also, every staff member (including administrative assistants who see children all day) should create a personal plan (see the templates below).

It's helpful to solicit the opinions of the staff regarding your organization's response. Many people on your staff may have already reported child abuse, whether at your organization or their previous job, and their concerns regarding the process are valid. Their experience dealing with local authorities can illuminate possible problems for your organization before they occur and guide you in creating policies and procedures.

Remember, you cannot require your staff to report to you in lieu of reporting to the authorities. This is illegal. You can ask your staff to include you in the report, but they don't have to do so. If your staff has not reported the abuse, you must then report it.

Encourage your staff to communicate with each other regarding child welfare. For example, if you have a fourth-grader and a second-grader who are siblings at your school, and the fourth-grade teacher notices signs of abuse on the older sibling, that teacher may want to alert the teacher of the younger sibling to keep an eye out. *This is especially important if one of the children is disabled or cannot communicate alone for any reason.* The teacher does not have to disclose whether or not a report was made. While you may encourage such communication, remind your staff that each of them still has individual reporting duties, and another teacher's observations or reports do not "cancel out" their duties.

During your training, some of your staff may want your reassurance that it is really okay to report abuse. Others may want clarification on an aspect of their duties. For example, someone may ask something like,

"My student was bitten severely by his uncle's dog three times last year. He had to have stitches twice. I told the parents about this and they didn't do anything. Should I report this to CPS?"

It is not your responsibility to know every aspect of your state's penal code, nor is it your staff's responsibility. Only a professional can answer these questions. Use this opportunity to direct your staff to call CPS and ask the representatives there. That's what CPS is there for. If your staff sees that you are not afraid to call CPS to ask such questions, they will be less hesitant to use the service themselves.

Response Plan Templates

Personal Response Plan

1. I learn of or grow suspicious of child abuse/teen relationship abuse.

2. I will report to _____. (List phone numbers.)

3. I   will   will not   report this to my supervisor. (Circle one.)

4. I will comply with agency responses.

5. I will meet with the child again if appropriate.

Organizational Response Plan

1. We learn of or grow suspicious of child abuse/teen relationship abuse.

2. The staff member directly involved will report to _____. (List phone numbers.)

3. Will the staff member report to our administration?   Yes   No

4. Which administrator will the staff member report to? _____

5. How will the administrator support the staff member?

APPENDIX II

Mandated Reporters in All 50 States

Other professions with mandated reporter responsibilities	States requiring mandated reports
All persons	DE, FL, ID, IN, KY, MD, MS, NE, NH, NJ, NM, NC, OK, RI, TN, TX, UT, WY
Neighbors	TN
Relatives	TN
Friends	TN
Any institution	NC
Any other person called upon to give aid or assistance to any child	AL
Anyone responsible for care or treatment of children	AZ, MO
Staff member of any public or private institution, school, facility, or agency	IN

Other professions with mandated reporter responsibilities	States requiring mandated reports
Camp administrators and counselors	VT
Coaches	IA
Employees of recreational or sports activities	HI
Responsible living skills program staff	WA
Employees or clinics that provide reproductive services	TX
Department of Human Services employees	AR
Employees of substance abuse programs	IA
Paid employees of domestic violence and sexual assault programs and drug and alcohol treatment facilities	AK
Domestic violence shelter employees and volunteers	AR, SD
Youth shelter workers	NV
Substance abuse treatment personnel	IL, SC
Substance abuse counselors	CT, MA, NV, NY, wi
Addiction or chemical dependency counselors	ND, SD
Sexual assault counselors	CT

Other professions with mandated reporter responsibilities	States requiring mandated reports
Battered women's counselors	CT
Domestic violence victim advocates	AZ
Victim advocates	CO
Child advocates	CT
Court Appointed Special Advocates	AR, CA, ME, OR, VA, WI
Guardian ad litem	ME, MT
Members of a child fatality review team or multidisciplinary child protection team	AK
Juvenile intake and assessment workers	KS
Computer technicians	SC
Internet service providers	MO
Commercial film or photograph processors	AK, CA, CO, IL, IA, LA, ME, MO, OK, SC
Private film or photograph processors	AK, SC
Persons who produce visual or printed matter	GA
Parents	AZ
Foster parents	AR

Other professions with mandated reporter responsibilities	States requiring mandated reports
Homemakers	IL, ME
Any adult with whom a child resides	WA
Ministers	MS
Clergy	AZ, AR, CA, CO, CT, IL, ME, MA, MI, MO, MT, NV, NH, NM, ND, OR, PA, VT, WV
Christian Science practitioners	AZ, AR, CO, IL, MA, MO, MT, NV, NH, NY, PA, SC, VA, WV
Religious healers	FL, MT, NV, ND, OH, SC, SD, TN, WV
Funeral home directors (and employees in SC)	IL, PA, SC
Attorneys	MS, NV, OH, OR
Prosecutors or District attorneys	AR, NY
Judges	AR, FL, NM, SC, TN, WV
Clerks/magistrates of district courts	MA, WV
Family law masters	WV
Firefighters	CA, CO, KS, MA, OR
Fire inspectors	ME
Probation, parole officers, court services officers	MA, MO, NV, SD, VT, VA

Other professions with mandated reporter responsibilities	States requiring mandated reports
Juvenile probation or detention officers	TX
Animal control officers	CA
Veterinarians	CO
Mediators	LA, VA, WI
Agents of human societies	ME, OH
Financial and employment planners	WI

Appendix III

Mandated Reporters by State

Each State and U.S. Territory has designated certain groups of people to be mandated by law to report child abuse. These people usually come into frequent contact with children as part of their profession.

Please note that many states require *all* citizens to report suspected abuse or neglect regardless of profession.

This information is adapted from the National Clearinghouse on Child Abuse and Neglect Information website.

Alabama
Statute: § 26-14-3(a); § 26-14-10
Professions That Must Report:

- Health care professionals

- Mental health professionals

- Social work professionals

- Education/child care professionals

- Law enforcement professionals

Others: Any other person called upon to give aid or assistance to any child
Standard: Known or suspected
Privileged Communications: Attorney/client

Alaska
Statute: § 47.17.020(a); § 47.17.023; § 47.17.060
Professions That Must Report:

- Health care professionals

- Mental health professionals

- Social work professionals

- Education/child care professionals

- Law enforcement professionals

Others:

- Paid employees of domestic violence and sexual assault programs and drug and alcohol treatment facilities

- Members of a child fatality review team or multidisciplinary child protection team

- Commercial or private film or photograph processors

Standard: Have reasonable cause to suspect
Privileged Communications: Not granted in statutes reviewed

American Samoa
Statute: § 45.2002
Professions That Must Report:

- Health care professionals

- Mental health professionals

- Social work professionals

- Education/child care professionals

Others:

- Medical examiner or coroner

- Christian Science practitioner

Standard:

- Have reasonable cause to know or suspect

- Have observed conditions which would reasonably result

Privileged Communications: Not addressed in statutes reviewed

Arizona
Statute: § 13-3620(A); § 8-805(B)-(C)
Professions That Must Report:

- Health care professionals

- Mental health professionals

- Social work professionals

- Education/child care professionals

- Law enforcement professionals

Others:

- Parents

- Anyone responsible for care or treatment of children

- Clergy/Christian Science practitioners

- Domestic violence victim advocates

Standard: Have reasonable grounds to believe
Privileged Communications:

- Clergy/penitent

- Attorney/client

Arkansas
Statute: § 12-12-507(b)-(c); § 12-12-518(b)(1)
Professions That Must Report:

- Health care professionals

- Mental health professionals
- Social work professionals
- Education/child care professionals
- Law enforcement professionals

Others:

- Prosecutors
- Judges
- Department of Human Services employees
- Domestic violence shelter employees and volunteers
- Foster parents
- Court Appointed Special Advocates
- Clergy/Christian Science practitioners

Standard:

- Have reasonable cause to suspect
- Have observed conditions which would reasonably result

Privileged Communications:

- Clergy/penitent
- Attorney/client

California
Statute: Penal Code § 11166(a), (c); § 11165.7(a)
Professions That Must Report:

- Health care professionals
- Mental health professionals
- Social work professionals

- Education/child care professionals
- Law enforcement professionals

Others:

- Firefighters
- Animal control officers
- Commercial film and photographic print processors
- Clergy
- Court Appointed Special Advocates

Standard:

- Have knowledge of or observe
- Know or reasonably suspect

Privileged Communications: Clergy/penitent

Colorado
Statute: § 19-3-304(1), (2), (2.5); § 19-3-311
Professions That Must Report:

- Health care professionals
- Mental health professionals
- Social work professionals
- Education/child care professionals
- Law enforcement professionals

Others:

- Christian Science practitioners
- Veterinarians
- Firefighters

- Victim advocates

- Commercial film and photographic print processors

- Clergy

Standard:

- Have reasonable cause to know or suspect

- Have observed conditions which would reasonably result

Privileged Communications: Clergy/penitent

Connecticut
Statute: § 17a-101(b); § 17a-101a
Professions That Must Report:

- Health care professionals

- Mental health professionals

- Social work professionals

- Education/child care professionals

- Law enforcement professionals

Others:

- Substance abuse counselors

- Sexual assault counselors

- Battered women's counselors

- Clergy

- Child advocates

Standard: Have reasonable cause to suspect or believe
Privileged Communications: Not addressed in statutes reviewed

Delaware
Statute: Tit. 16 § 903; § 909
Professions That Must Report:

- Health care professionals

- Mental health professionals

- Social work professionals

- Education/child care professionals

- All persons

Others: Not addressed in statutes reviewed
Standard: Know or in good faith suspect
Privileged Communications:

- Attorney/client

- Clergy/penitent

District of Columbia
Statute: § 4-1321.02(a), (b), (d); § 4-1321.05
Professions That Must Report:

- Health care professionals

- Mental health professionals

- Social work professionals

- Education/child care professionals

- Law enforcement professionals

Others: Not addressed in statutes reviewed
Standard: Know or have reasonable cause to suspect
Privileged Communications: Not granted in statutes reviewed

Florida
Statute: § 39.201(1); § 39.204
Professions That Must Report:

- Health care professionals

- Mental health professionals

- Social work professionals

- Education/child care professionals

- Law enforcement professionals

- All persons

Others:

- Judges

- Religious healers

Standard: Know or have reasonable cause to suspect
Privileged Communications: Attorney/client

Georgia
Statute: § 19-7-5(c)(1), (g); § 16-12-100(c)
Professions That Must Report:

- Health care professionals

- Mental health professionals

- Social work professionals

- Education/child care professionals

- Law enforcement professionals

Others: Persons who produce visual or printed matter
Standard: Have reasonable cause to believe
Privileged Communications: Not granted in statutes reviewed

Guam
Statute: Tit. 19, § 13201
Professions That Must Report:

- Health care professionals
- Mental health professionals
- Social work professionals
- Education/child care professionals
- Law enforcement professionals

Others:

- Christian Science practitioners
- Commercial film and photographic print processors

Standard:

- Have reason to suspect
- Have knowledge or observe

Privileged Communications: Not granted in statutes reviewed

Hawaii
Statute: § 350-1.1(a); § 350-5
Professions That Must Report:

- Health care professionals
- Mental health professionals
- Social work professionals
- Education/child care professionals
- Law enforcement professionals

Others: Employees of recreational or sports activities
Standard: Have reason to believe
Privileged Communications: Not granted in statutes reviewed

Idaho
Statute: § 16-1619(a), (c); § 16-1620
Professions That Must Report:

- Health care professionals

- Mental health professionals

- Social work professionals

- Education/child care professionals

- Law enforcement professionals

- All persons

Others: Not addressed in statutes reviewed
Standard:

- Have reason to believe

- Have observed conditions which would reasonably result

Privileged Communications: Clergy/penitent Attorney/client

Illinois
Statute: 325 ILCS § 5/4
Professions That Must Report:

- Health care professionals

- Mental health professionals

- Social work professionals

- Education/child care professionals

- Law enforcement professionals

Others:

- Homemakers

- Substance abuse treatment personnel

- Christian Science practitioners

- Funeral home directors

- Commercial film and photographic print processors

- Clergy

Standard: Have reasonable cause to believe
Privileged Communications: Clergy/penitent

Indiana
Statute: § 31-33-5-1; § 31-33-5-2; § 31-32-11-1
Professions That Must Report:

- Health care professionals

- Mental health professionals

- Social work professionals

- Education/child care professionals

- Law enforcement professionals

- All persons

Others: Staff member of any public or private institution, school, facility, or agency
Standard: Have reason to believe
Privileged Communications: Not granted in statutes reviewed

Iowa
Statute: § 232.69(1)(a)-(b); § 728.14(1); § 232.74
Professions That Must Report:

- Health care professionals

- Mental health professionals

- Social work professionals

- Education/child care professionals

- Law enforcement professionals

Others:

- Commercial film and photographic print processors

- Employees of substance abuse programs

- Coaches

Standard: Reasonably believe
Privileged Communications: Not granted in statutes reviewed

Kansas
Statute: § 38-1522(a), (b)
Professions That Must Report:

- Health care professionals

- Mental health professionals

- Social work professionals

- Education/child care professionals

- Law enforcement professionals

Others:

- Firefighters

- Juvenile intake and assessment workers

Standard: Have reason to suspect
Privileged Communications: Not addressed in statutes reviewed

Kentucky
Statute: § 620.030(1), (2); § 620.050(3)
Professions That Must Report:

- Health care professionals

- Mental health professionals

- Social work professionals

- Education/child care professionals

- Law enforcement professionals

- All persons

Others: Not addressed in statutes reviewed
Standard: Know or have reasonable cause to believe
Privileged Communications:

- Attorney/client

- Clergy/penitent

Louisiana
Statute: Ch. Code art. § 603(13); § 609(A)(1); § 610(F)
Professions That Must Report:

- Health care professionals

- Mental health professionals

- Social work professionals

- Education/child care professionals

- Law enforcement professionals

Others:

- Commercial film or photographic print processors

- Mediators

Standard: Have cause to believe
Privileged Communications: Clergy, Christian Science practi-tioner/penitent

Maine
Statute: Tit. 22, § 4011-A(1); § 4015
Professions That Must Report:

- Health care professionals

- Mental health professionals

- Social work professionals

- Education/child care professionals

- Law enforcement professionals

Others:

- Guardians ad litem and Court Appointed Special Advocates

- Fire inspectors

- Commercial film processors

- Homemakers

- Humane agents

- Clergy

Standard: Know or have reasonable cause to suspect
Privileged Communications: Clergy/penitent

Maryland
Statute: Family Law § 5-704(a); § 5-705(a)(1)
Professions That Must Report:

- Health care professionals

- Mental health professionals

- Social work professionals

- Education/child care professionals

- Law enforcement professionals

- All persons

Others: Not addressed in statutes reviewed
Standard: Have reason to believe
Privileged Communications:

- Attorney/client

- Clergy/penitent

Massachusetts
Statute: Ch. 119, § 51A; § 51B
Professions That Must Report:

- Health care professionals

- Mental health professionals

- Social work professionals

- Education/child care professionals

- Law enforcement professionals

Others:

- Drug and alcoholism counselors

- Probation and parole officers

- Clerks/magistrates of district courts

- Firefighters

- Clergy/Christian Science practitioners

Standard: Have reasonable cause to believe
Privileged Communications: Clergy/penitent

Michigan
Statute: § 722.623 (1), (8); § 722.631
Professions That Must Report:

- Health care professionals

- Mental health professionals

- Social work professionals

- Education/child care professionals

- Law enforcement professionals

Others: Clergy
Standard: Have reasonable cause to suspect
Privileged Communications:

- Attorney/client

- Clergy/penitent

Minnesota
Statute: § 626.556 Subd. 3(a), 8
Professions That Must Report:

- Health care professionals

- Mental health professionals

- Social work professionals

- Education/child care professionals

- Law enforcement professionals

Others: Not addressed in statutes reviewed
Standard: Know or have reason to believe
Privileged Communications: Clergy/penitent

Mississippi
Statute: § 43-21-353(1)
Professions That Must Report:

- Health care professionals
- Mental health professionals
- Social work professionals
- Education/child care professionals
- Law enforcement professionals
- All persons

Others:

- Attorneys
- Ministers

Standard: Have reasonable cause to suspect
Privileged Communications: Not addressed in statutes reviewed

Missouri
Statute: § 210.115(1); § 568.110; § 210.140
Professions That Must Report:

- Health care professionals
- Mental health professionals
- Social work professionals
- Education/child care professionals
- Law enforcement professionals

Others:

- Persons with responsibility for care of children
- Christian Science practitioners

- Probation/parole officers
- Commercial film processors
- Internet service providers
- Clergy

Standard:

- Have reasonable cause to suspect
- Have observed conditions which would reasonably result

Privileged Communications:

- Attorney/client
- Clergy/penitent

Montana
Statute: § 41-3-201(1)-(2), (4)
Professions That Must Report:

- Health care professionals
- Mental health professionals
- Social work professionals
- Education/child care professionals
- Law enforcement professionals

Others:

- Guardians ad litem
- Clergy
- Religious healers
- Christian Science practitioners

Standard: Know or have reasonable cause to suspect
Privileged Communications: Clergy/penitent

Nebraska
Statute: § 28-711(1); § 28-714
Professions That Must Report:

- Health care professionals

- Social work professionals

- Education/child care professionals

- All persons

Others: Not addressed in statutes reviewed

Standard:

- Have reasonable cause to believe

- Have observed conditions which would reasonably result

Privileged Communications: Not granted in statutes reviewed

Nevada
Statute: § 432B.220(3), (5); § 432B.250
Professions That Must Report:

- Health care professionals

- Mental health professionals

- Social work professionals

- Education/child care professionals

- Law enforcement professionals

Others:

- Religious healers

- Alcohol/drug abuse counselors
- Clergy/Christian Science practitioners
- Probation officers
- Attorneys
- Youth shelter workers

Standard: Know or have reason to believe
Privileged Communications:

- Clergy/penitent
- Attorney/client

New Hampshire
Statute: § 169-C:29; § 169-C:32
Professions That Must Report:

- Health care professionals
- Mental health professionals
- Social work professionals
- Education/child care professionals
- Law enforcement professionals
- All persons

Others:

- Christian Science practitioners
- Clergy

Standard: Have reason to suspect
Privileged Communications:

- Attorney/client
- Clergy/penitent privilege denied

New Jersey
Statute: § 9:6-8.10
Professions That Must Report:
All persons
Others: Not addressed in statutes reviewed
Standard: Have reasonable cause to believe
Privileged Communications: Not addressed in statutes reviewed

New Mexico
Statute: § 32A-4-3(A); § 32A-4-5(A)
Professions That Must Report:

- Health care professionals

- Mental health professionals

- Social work professionals

- Education/child care professionals

- Law enforcement professionals

- All persons

Others:

- Judges

- Clergy

Standard: Know or have reasonable suspicion
Privileged Communications: Clergy/penitent

New York
Statute: Soc. Serv. Law § 413(1)
Professions That Must Report:

- Health care professionals

- Mental health professionals

- Social work professionals

- Education/child care professionals

- Law enforcement professionals

Others:

- Alcoholism/substance abuse counselors

- District attorneys

- Christian Science practitioners

Standard: Have reasonable cause to suspect
Privileged Communications: Not addressed in statutes reviewed

North Carolina
Statute: § 7B-301; § 7B-310
Professions That Must Report:
All persons
Others: Any institution
Standard: Have cause to suspect
Privileged Communications:

- Attorney/client

- Clergy/penitent privilege denied

North Dakota
Statute: § 50-25.1-03; § 50-25.1-10
Professions That Must Report:

- Health care professionals

- Mental health professionals

- Social work professionals

- Education/child care professionals

- Law enforcement professionals

Others:

- Clergy

- Religious healers

- Addiction counselors

Standard: Have knowledge of or reasonable cause to suspect
Privileged Communications:

- Clergy/penitent

- Attorney/client

Northern Mariana Islands
Statute: Tit. 6, § 5313(a); § 5316
Professions That Must Report:

- Health care professionals

- Education/child care professionals

- Law enforcement professionals

Others:

- Medical examiners/coroners

- Religious healers

Standard: Know or have reasonable cause to suspect
Privileged Communications: Attorney/client

Ohio
Statute: § 2151.421(A)(1), (A)(2), (G)(1)(b)
Professions That Must Report:

- Health care professionals

- Mental health professionals

- Social work professionals

- Education/child care professionals

Others:

- Attorneys

- Religious healers

- Agents of humane societies

Standard: Know or suspect
Privileged Communications:

- Attorney/client

- Physician/patient

Oklahoma
Statute: Tit. 10, § 7103(A)(1); § 7104; § 7113
Professions That Must Report:

- Health care professionals

- Education/child care professionals

- All persons

Others: Commercial film and photographic print processors

Standard: Have reason to believe
Privileged Communications: Not granted in statutes reviewed

Oregon
Statute: § 419B.005(3); § 419B.010(1)

- Health care professionals

- Mental health professionals

- Social work professionals

- Education/child care professionals

- Law enforcement professionals

Others:

- Attorneys
- Clergy
- Firefighters
- Court Appointed Special Advocates

Standard: Have reasonable cause to believe
Privileged Communications:

- Mental health/patient
- Clergy/penitent
- Attorney/client

Pennsylvania
Statute: 23 Pa. § 6311(a), (b)
Professions That Must Report:

- Health care professionals
- Mental health professionals
- Social work professionals
- Education/child care professionals
- Law enforcement professionals

Others:

- Funeral directors
- Christian Science practitioners
- Clergy

Standard: Have reasonable cause to suspect
Privileged Communications: Clergy/penitent

Puerto Rico
Statute: Tit. 8, § 441a; § 441b
Professions That Must Report:

- Health care professionals
- Mental health professionals
- Social work professionals
- Education/child care professionals
- Law enforcement professionals
- All persons

Others:

- Professionals or public officials
- Processors of film or photographs

Standard:

- Should know or have knowledge of
- Suspects
- Observes

Privileged Communications: Not addressed in statutes reviewed

Rhode Island
Statute: § 40-11-3(a); § 40-11-6(a); § 40-11-11
Professions That Must Report:

- Health care professionals
- All persons

Others: Not addressed in statutes reviewed
Standard: Have reasonable cause to know or suspect
Privileged Communications:

- Attorney/client

- Clergy/penitent privilege denied

South Carolina
Statute: § 20-7-510(A); § 20-7-550
Professions That Must Report:

- Health care professionals

- Mental health professionals

- Social work professionals

- Education/child care professionals

- Law enforcement professionals

Others:

- Judges

- Funeral home directors and employees

- Christian Science practitioners

- Film processors

- Religious healers

- Substance abuse treatment staff

- Computer technicians

Standard: Have reason to believe
Privileged Communications:

- Attorney/client

- Clergy/penitent

South Dakota
Statute: § 26-8A-3; § 26-8A-15
Professions That Must Report:

- Health care professionals

- Mental health professionals

- Social work professionals

- Education/child care professionals

- Law enforcement professionals

Others:

- Chemical dependency counselors

- Religious healers

- Parole or court services officers

- Employees of domestic abuse shelters

Standard: Have reasonable cause to suspect
Privileged Communications: Not granted in statutes reviewed

Tennessee
Statute: § 37-1-403(a); § 37-1-605(a); § 37-1-411
Professions That Must Report:

- Health care professionals

- Mental health professionals

- Social work professionals

- Education/child care professionals

- Law enforcement professionals

- All persons

Others:

- Judges
- Neighbors
- Relatives
- Friends
- Religious healers

Standard:

- Knowledge of/reasonably know
- Have reasonable cause to suspect

Privileged Communications: Not granted in statutes reviewed

Texas
Statute: Family Code § 261.101(a)-(c); § 261.102
Professions That Must Report:

- Health care professionals
- Education/child care professionals
- All persons

Others:

- Juvenile probation or detention officers
- Employees or clinics that provide reproductive services

Standard: Have cause to believe
Privileged Communications: Clergy/penitent privilege denied

Utah
Statute: § 62A-4a-403(1)-(3); § 62A-4a-412(5)
Professions That Must Report:

- Health care professionals

- All persons

Others: Not addressed in statutes reviewed
Standard:

- Have reason to believe

- Have observed conditions which would reasonably result

Privileged Communications: Clergy/penitent

Vermont
Statute: Tit. 33, § 4913(a), (f)-(h)
Professions That Must Report:

- Health care professionals

- Mental health professionals

- Social work professionals

- Education/child care professionals

- Law enforcement professionals

Others:

- Camp administrators and counselors

- Probation officers

- Clergy

Standard: Have reasonable cause to believe
Privileged Communications: Clergy/penitent

Virgin Islands
Statute: Tit. 5, § 2533(a); § 2538
Professions That Must Report:

- Health care professionals

- Mental health professionals

- Social work professionals

- Education/child care professionals

- Law enforcement professionals

Others: Not addressed in statutes reviewed
Standard:

- Have reasonable cause to suspect

- Observe conditions which would reasonably result

Privileged Communications: Attorney/client

Virginia
Statute: § 63.2-1509(A); § 63.2-1519
Professions That Must Report:

- Health care professionals

- Mental health professionals

- Social work professionals

- Education/child care professionals

- Law enforcement professionals

Others:

- Mediators

- Christian Science practitioners

- Probation officers

- Court Appointed Special Advocates

Standard: Have reason to suspect
Privileged Communications: Not granted in statutes reviewed

Washington
Statute: § 26.44.030 (1), (2); § 26.44.060(3)
Professions That Must Report:

- Health care professionals

- Mental health professionals

- Social work professionals

- Education/child care professionals

- Law enforcement professionals

Others:

- Any adult with whom a child resides

- Responsible living skills program staff

Standard: Have reasonable cause to believe
Privileged Communications: Not granted in statutes reviewed

West Virginia
Statute: § 49-6A-2; § 49-6A-7
Professions That Must Report:

- Health care professionals

- Mental health professionals

- Social work professionals

- Education/child care professionals

- Law enforcement professionals

Others:

- Clergy

- Religious healers

- Judges, family law masters or magistrates

- Christian Science practitioners

Standard:

- Reasonable cause to suspect

- When believe

- Have observed

Privileged Communications:

- Attorney/client

- Clergy/penitent privilege denied

Wisconsin
Statute: § 48.981(2), (2m)(c)-(e)
Professions That Must Report:

- Health care professionals

- Mental health professionals

- Social work professionals

- Education/child care professionals

- Law enforcement professionals

Others:

- Alcohol or drug abuse counselors

- Mediators

- Financial and employment planners

- Court Appointed Special Advocates

Standard:

- Have reasonable cause to suspect

- Have reason to believe

Privileged Communications: Not addressed in statutes reviewed

Wyoming
Statute: § 14-3-205(a); § 14-3-210
Professions That Must Report:
All persons
Others: Not addressed in statutes reviewed
Standard:

- Know or have reasonable cause to believe or suspect

- Have observed conditions which would reasonably result

Privileged Communications:

- Attorney/client

- Physician/patient

- Clergy/penitent

APPENDIX IV

Resources

In an emergency, dial 9-1-1.

National Child Abuse Reporting Hotline:
1-800-4-A-CHILD
1-800-422-4453

The National Child Abuse Reporting hotline is maintained by ChildHelp USA and is available 24 hours a day, 7 days a week. Operators will give you your local telephone number for reporting abuse. They also provide assistance and consultations to professionals in fields that have close contact with children and that are usually mandated to report child abuse (ChildHelp USA, 2004).

Community Resources
Use this section to write in other local numbers and resources in your area.

Resource	Phone/Fax	Notes

References

[1] The Public Broadcasting Service (2004). Juggling Work and Family with Hedrick Smith. National Statistics: Snapshots of work and family in America. The Public Broadcasting Service. Retrieved on May 25, 2004 from http://www.pbs.org/workfamily/discussion_snapshots.html.

[2] The Public Broadcasting Service (2004). Juggling Work and Family with Hedrick Smith. National Statistics: Snapshots of work and family in America. The Public Broadcasting Service. Retrieved on May 25, 2004 from http://www.pbs.org/workfamily/discussion_snapshots.html.

[3] National Clearinghouse on Child Abuse and Neglect Information. "Mandatory Reporters of Child Abuse and Neglect." http://nccanch.acf.hhs.gov/general/legal/statutes/sag/manda.pdf (Current through June 2003).

[4] National Clearinghouse on Child Abuse and Neglect Information (2004). *What is Child Abuse and Neglect?* Retrieved July 12, 2004 from http://nccanch.acf.hhs.gov/pubs/factsheets/whatiscan.pdf

[5] U.S. Department of Justice—Bureau of Justice Statistics (2003 February). *Intimate Partner Violence, 1993–2001.* Retrieved June 27, 2004 from http://www.ojp.usdoj.gov/bjs/pub/pdf/ipv01.pdf

[6] Perry BD: Neurobiological sequelae of childhood trauma: post-traumatic stress disorders in children. In M. Murberg (Ed.), Catecholamines in Post-traumatic Stress Disorder: Emerging

Concepts. Washington, D.C. American Psychiatric Press, 1994a, pp 253-276.

[7] Perry BD, Pollard RA, Baker WL, et al: Continuous heartrate monitoring in maltreated children [Abstract]. Annual Meeting of the American Academy of Child and Adolescent Psychiatry, New Research, 1995.

[8] Perry BD: Incubated in terror: neurodevelopmental factors in the 'cycle of violence' In: Children, Youth and Violence: The Search for Solutions (J Osofsky, Ed.). Guilford Press, New York, 1997, pp 124-148.

[9] Perry BD: Memories of fear: how the brain stores and retrieves physiologic states, feelings, behaviors and thoughts from traumatic events: In: Splintered Reflections: Images of the Body in Trauma (JM Goodwin and R. Attias, Ed.). Basic Books, 1999, pp 26-47.

[10] Lauder JM: Neurotransmitters as morphogens. Progress in Brain Research 73:365-388, 1988.

[11] McAllister AK, Katz LC, Lo DC: Neurotrophins and synaptic plasticity. Annual Rev Neuroscience 22:295-318, 1999.

[12] Brown JW: Morphogenesis and mental process. Development and Psychopathology 6:551-563, 1994.

[13] Courchesne E, Chisum H, Townsend J: Neural activity-dependent brain changes in development: implications for psychopathology. Development and Psychopathology 6(4):697-722, 1994.

[14] McAllister AK, Katz LC, Lo DC: Neurotrophins and synaptic plasticity. Annu Rev Neurosci 22:295-318, 1999.

[15] Perry BD: Memories of fear: how the brain stores and retrieves physiologic states, feelings, behaviors and thoughts from traumatic events: In: Splintered Reflections: Images of the Body in Trauma (JM Goodwin and R. Attias, Ed.). Basic Books, 1999, pp 26-47.

[16] Perry BD: Incubated in terror: neurodevelopmental factors in the 'cycle of violence' In: Children, Youth and Violence: The Search for Solutions (J Osofsky, Ed.). Guilford Press, New York, 1997, pp 124-148.

[17] Perry BD, Azad I: Post-traumatic stress disorders in children and adolescents. Current Opinion in Pediatrics 11:121-132, 1999.

[18] U.S. Department of Health and Human Services (2002). Study Shows Positive Results from Early Headstart Program. Retrieved on June 25, 2004 from http://www.hhs.gov/news/press/2002pres/20020603.html.

[19] U.S. Department of Health and Human Services, Administration for Children and Families (2000). Child Welfare Outcomes 2000: Annual Report. Retrieved November 12, 2005 from http://www.acf.hhs.gov/programs/cb/publications/cwoo/chaps/toc.htm.

[20] Crime and Prevention Center, California Attorney General's Office (2003). Abuse of Children with Disabilities. (Flyer.)

[21] Diamond, Marion, Ph.D., and Hopson, Janet. *The Magic Trees of the Mind.* New York: Penguin Putnam, 1998.

[22] Diamond, Marion, Ph.D., and Hopson, Janet. *The Magic Trees of the Mind.* New York: Penguin Putnam, 1998.

[23] Diamond, Marion, Ph.D., and Hopson, Janet. *The Magic Trees of the Mind.* New York: Penguin Putnam, 1998.

[24] Centers for Disease Control and Prevention. Youth risk behavior surveillance—United States, 1999. In: CDC Surveillance Summaries, June 9, 2000. MMWR 2000. Retrieved October 27, 2005 from http://www.cdc.gov/mmwr/preview/mmwrhtml/ss4905a1.htm.

[25] National Clearinghouse on Child Abuse and Neglect Information (2004). *What is Child Abuse and Neglect?* Retrieved July 12, 2004 from http://nccanch.acf.hhs.gov/pubs/factsheets/whatiscan.pdf

[26] Nichols, L. (1994). Preschool Sexuality Guide for Parents. PROSTEPP. Retrieved on August 4, 2004 from http://danenet.wicip.org/dcccrsa/saissues/prostepp/page4.html.

[27] The British Broadcasting Company (2004). Talking to Children about Abuse. Retrieved on August 4, 2004, from http://www.bbc.co.uk/parenting/your_kids/safety_talking.shtml.

[28] Helpguide (2004). Domestic Violence: Types, signs, symptoms, causes, and effects. Retrieved on August 4, 2004, from http://www.helpguide.org/mental/spousal_abuse.htm.

[29] Nichols, L. (1994). Preschool Sexuality Guide for Parents. PROSTEPP. Retrieved on August 4, 2004 from http://danenet.wicip.org/dcccrsa/saissues/prostepp/page4.html.

[30] National Clearinghouse on Child Abuse and Neglect Information. "Mandatory Reporters of Child Abuse and Neglect." http://nccanch.acf.hhs.gov/general/legal/statutes/sag/manda.pdf (Current through June 2003).

[31] National Clearinghouse on Child Abuse and Neglect Information (2004). How Does the Child Welfare System Work? U.S. Department of Health and Human Services. Retrieved on December 9, 2004 from http://nccanch.acf.hhs.gov/pubs/factsheets/cpswork.pdf

[32] WomensLaw.org (2004). What Is a Protective or Restraining Order? Retrieved June 27, 2004 from <ins>www.womenslaw.org/ more info.htm</ins> and <ins>www.womenslaw.org/teens.htm</ins>.

Other Works Consulted

1. Ballie, R. (December 2001). Spanking Study Gets Big Play in the Media. *Monitor on Psychology*, v. 32 n.11. The American Psychological Association. Retrieved on December 8, 2004 from http://www.apa.org/monitor/dec01/spanking.html.

2. ChildHelp USA, 2004. Report Abuse. Retrieved on August 4, 2004 from http://www.childhelpusa.org/report_hotline.htm.

3. *Crawford v. Washington.* (02-9410) 541 U.S. 36. 147 Wash. 2004. Retrieved on November 15, 2005 from http://www.law.cornell.edu/supct/html/02-9410.ZO.html.

4. Food and Nutrition Services (2003). The National School Lunch Program Background and Development. United States Department of Agriculture. Retrieved on June 25, 2004 from http://www.fns.usda.gov/cnd/Lunch/About Lunch/ProgramHistory_8.htm.

5. National Clearinghouse on Child Abuse and Neglect Information (2002). *Child Maltreatment 2002: Summary of Key Findings.* Retrieved June 27, 2004 from http://nccanch.acf.hhs.gov/pubs/factsheets/canstats.pdf

6. MedicineNet.com (2002). Child Abuse. Retrieved June 26, 2004 from http://www.medicinenet.com/Child_Abuse/page1.htm.

7. Perry BD, Pollard R, Blakely T, et al: Childhood trauma, the neurobiology of adaptation and 'use-dependent' development of the brain: how "states" become "traits"'. Infant Mental Health Journal 16(4):271-291, 1995.

8. Perry BD, Pollard R: Homeostasis, stress, trauma, and adaptation: a neurodevelopmental view of childhood trauma.

Child and Adolescent Psychiatric Clinics of North America 7(1):33-51, 1998.

9. U.S. Department of Health and Human Services (2002). Study Shows Positive Results from Early Headstart Program. Retrieved on June 25, 2004 from http://www.hhs.gov/news/press/2002pres/20020603.html.

10. U.S. Department of Health and Human Services, Administration for Children and Families, Administration on Children, Youth and Families, Children's Bureau, Office on Child Abuse and Neglect. *Emerging Practices in the Prevention of Child Abuse and Neglect*, (2003). Retrieved on June 26, 2004 from http://nccanch.acf.hhs.gov/topics/prevention/emerging/nature.cfm

11. U.S. Department of Justice—Bureau of Justice Statistics (2003 February). *Intimate Partner Violence, 1993–2001*. Retrieved June 27, 2004 from http://www.ojp.usdoj.gov/bjs/pub/pdf/ipv01.pdf

Acknowledgments

We are indebted to the researchers whose contributions to the field of child welfare we have learned so much from. We also wholeheartedly thank Pamela Iles, Dr. Jill Murray, and Dr. Tracy Kemble for their support.

From Jesse: Thank you to my wonderful husband, Enrique, my beautiful Sophia, my parents, and Lucy for all your love and support while I wrote this book. Also, Aimee Bender, Rob Spillman, Sage Vanden Heuvel, Carol Olson, Olga García Gutiérrez, and Steven Cox—I appreciate all you've done for me as a writer.

From Kathy: For DTN with my deepest love, gratitude, and appreciation.

From Johanna: Thank you to my Lord and Savior Jesus Christ and to my loving parents, Dr. and Mrs. Kye Kim.

About the Authors

Jesse Rutherford, Kathleen Nickerson, PhD, and Johanna Kim, Esq., have extensive experience helping others to recognize and perform their mandated reporting duties. As a professional writer and curriculum developer, Jesse Rutherford has prepared materials for the United States Department of Justice on recognizing and responding to teen dating violence. As a licensed clinical psychologist, Kathleen Nickerson has spoken to countless professionals about their concerns about reporting abuse and she has given over 80 presentations at a wide variety of conferences, local radio shows, and television programs on the topic of responding to abuse. As an attorney, Johanna Kim has presented to hundreds of mandated reporters about the legal aspects of their reporting duties.

Jesse Rutherford Writing Services: stilljesse@yahoo.com.

Dr. Kathleen Nickerson, Licensed Clinical Psychologist: drkathynickerson@yahoo.com.

978-0-595-38122-7
0-595-38122-7